An Original Car Guy

The E. B. Gallaher Story

- **By djv murphy**

Greci

Happy 90TH !

DJVMurphy

Acknowledgements

A great deal of help was received by the author with research for this biography and a number of people were most gracious in their assistance.

- Celia Maddox, President of the Friends of Cranbury Park in Norwalk, Connecticut and Holly Cuzzone, a Norwalk Historical Commissioner.
- The Alumnae Office and Library Staff at The Stevens Institute including Executive Director Anita Lang, Loretta Brisette, Michael Smullen, Doris A. Oliver, and Adam Winger.
- Lori B. Bessler of the Wisconsin Historical Society
- Andre'e Vlaentino-Long of the Norwalk-Wilton Probate District
- Paige Plant of the Detroit Public Library
- Richard Prego, The Stevens Institute of Technology [archives]
- Jeannie C. Sherman, History and Genealogy Unit, Connecticut State Library.
- Mark Theobold of the website Coachbuilt.com
- Dan Vaughn of the website Conceptcarz.com
- Wikipedia, The Free Encyclopedia Wikipedia.org
- A very special thank you to my editor and friend Rosemary Carroll.

EDWARD BEACH GALLAHER
[circa 1947]

DEDICATION

To the men and women who through their imagination, creativity and stick-to-itiveness invent a new or better way of doing things.

*There are those who think
and those who act.
There are those who do
and those who don't.*

*There are those who think
and those who produce.
There are those who invent
and those who implement.*

*Then there are the entrepreneurs
who turn imagination into reality and
take inventions into everyday practicality.*

djv murphy ©

> "We Americans, who are now in our 70's have had opportunity for intimate knowledge of and in many cases opportunity to take part in creating more inventions an more developments than probably any others ever have seen and known."

Edward Beach Gallaher in his Newcomen Speech circa 1947

CHAPTER ONE
The Early Years

Edward Beach [E. B.] Gallaher was an inventor and entrepreneur; a car builder and a car racer. Truly an original "car guy" by any definition of the phrase. Perhaps he could also be called a practical philosopher.

In a speech he gave many decades ago, one might conclude that this unique person was certainly a man for his time.

The year was 1947 and the setting was the Pierre Hotel in New York City. The occasion was a meeting of the Newcomen Society of England.

The audience consisted of the crème de la crème of business, automotive and education leaders who were surprised and entertained by an astounding speech presented by an 73-year-old man.

During his appearance in front of this impressive gathering, he outlined and highlighted a number of inventions, which took place during his lifetime. It was an incredible period during the 1880's through the 1920's in America.

The Newcomen Society* speech also highlighted the most interesting events in the life of this one man. A life devoted to trying and failing, trying again and succeeding, which changed the course of his life. The speech was published by Mr. Gallaher in 1947, *"Progress in America which I have seen --- since the 1880's."* [permission to abstract with credit to the author.]

E. B.'s book showed a man who started out with an well-honed interest in mechanics, engines, automobiles, boating, inventions, and then organized a number of companies. He could easily have been called a pioneer entrepreneur.

Newcomen Society INFO in Appendix Two

—

Even though he came from wealth, along the way he accumulated his own significant financial resource and a political philosophy which today would be referred to as "right of Attila The Hun."

To his dying day, he loved his alma mater The Stevens Institute located in Hoboken, New Jersey. His final wish was to leave his life savings and property to this institution in order to carry on research programs and establish such a facility on his Connecticut estate.

The wish however was never carried out. It seems as if his bequest disappeared in the bowels of The Stevens Institute and to this day the money and its use and whereabouts remain a mystery.

His story begins when he was just a tyke growing independent in his teen years and then on into his "car guy" years. Along the way he somehow became fiercely libertarian and espoused his political leanings and beliefs in a most unusual way. With his love of writing, he developed his own newsletter, which became very popular with those that shared his conservative views and opinions.

Born in 1873 to an established and wealthy family, Edward Beach Gallaher considered this fact both a blessing and a curse. He once remarked about it and expressed his mixed feelings. This following quote captures his thoughts on the matter:

> *"The good fortune, as well as misfortune, befell me of being born to a socially prominent family.....good fortune because it brought personal contact with the outstanding men of the past generation, and to have known them at the very height of their active careers.......at a time when everyone was talking about them.......and misfortune because of natural impediments to independently making my own way in the world."*

E. B. Gallaher describing his conflicting thoughts

After his birth in Paris to Samuel Capp Gallaher and his wife Julia Ann [Beach] he spent his childhood there and also in Switzerland.

He came from a long line of educated and successful men, including Elihu Yale, the founder of Yale University and former Governor of the East India Company of London, England.

His grandfather was an inventor of machinery during the 1860's, which was still in use almost 100 years later. Grandfather Moses Yale Beach was also the owner of the *New York Sun* newspaper and founded the *Pony Express* and the *Associated Press.*

An uncle, Alfred E. Beach founded the magazine *Scientific American* and served as its editor for 50 years. "Uncle Alfred" was considered an exceptional inventive genius.

Among his inventions, as referenced in the biographical sketch in E. B.'s book, were the typewriter and the Beach Hydraulic Tunneling Shield used by engineers through out the world.

His uncle also built and operated a short subway in New York, which ran from the present site of the Central Post Office to Chambers Street in lower Manhattan.

The compressed-air delivery of mail [used later by department stores and offices to send inter-office mail and newspapers through tubes installed on each floor] was one of the Uncle's inventions.

After his family returned from Europe in the 1880's, E. B. spent his youth in preparatory schools in New York.

His self-description included the phrase, "precocious kid" since he said he was always working with tools and interested in everything new.

At age 14 he became a member of the well respected American Society of Amateur Photographers. It didn't hurt that his cousin founded the A.S.A.P. organization.

In his teens he was an avid photographer and inventor as well. He bought an "English Ross" lens and proceeded to build his own camera [there were none to be had on the market at that juncture].

He was so good at the process of "wet-plate" image reproduction that he won a number of club prizes. This was before the day of dry plate photographic reproduction.

The Statue of Liberty also figured in the young life of E. B.

President Grover Cleveland attended the dedication ceremony in late 1886. But a few years later E. B.'s photo club was reported to have photographed another ceremony.

His photographer's club rented a small boat as their first club outing. They went out into the New York Harbor and to the now site of the Statue of Liberty.

They photographed a reception of a French Admiral who had led the transport of the Statue's transatlantic trip. A reception was held at the base of the pedestal where E. B. took photographs of the ceremony.

It seems as if they are the only photographic images of the historic presentation.

Later and after saving his money, he had his sights set on a more formal engineering education and sought enrollment at The Stevens Institute of Technology in New Jersey, across the river from New York City.

Edwin A. Stevens, who lived in Hoboken, left his estate to create the Institute in 1870 and it was thought to be the first such engineering college in the country.

The Institute made a great impression on E. B. and through his work in photography he saved enough money to pay most of his way through the Steven's program.

Paying his own way was a turning point in his life, as being independent and self-sufficient were driving forces in his life.

He did not change his personal assessment of having been born into wealth to be an impediment towards his goal of independence.

In his Newcomen Society remarks E. B. noted that he invented a new process by accident, which turned a photograph into a drawing.

"Through a lucky accident, I found myself working on some silver prints which I had just completed when I knocked a bottle over and spilled its contents upon my new prints. Wherever the liquid touched, the paper became snow white. Wondering whether this bleaching solution would affect India ink, I tried it. It did not," he added.

"Then I made a print and outlined the subject in India ink, then bleached away the print, and I had a drawing which had the accuracy and perspective of a photograph."

E. B. describing how he made an astounding discovery.

It is reported that this accidental invention proved to be a break through for his talents. The managing editor of the New York World Newspaper then hired him as the paper's first official news photographer even giving him status as a reporter.

This first illustration was a picture of the offices of Thomas C. Platt, President of the United States Express Company. E. B. had called him as a friend of the family and asked permission to photograph his beautiful offices. He acquiesced.

He then took the photograph to an artist-friend who outlined the photo in India ink. E. B. then bleached away the photo and created an accurate pen-and-ink drawing, which looked like a photograph.

The picture appeared in the *World* in December 1889 making it the first illustration ever to be made directly from a photograph.

As a result of E. B.'s success, the newspaper established an art department and several employees were added to the staff to draw over the photographs delivered by E. B.

Incredibly, he was only sixteen years of age and the year was more than a decade away from the 20th Century. For E. B., this was just the beginning of his life long achievements.

> *"Thus there were impractical incandescent lamps before Edison. Edison made them practical and rightfully is hailed as the inventor. There were steam carriages 120 years before the gasolene [sic] engine was developed, which in turn, made the automobile possible."*

E. B. describing how inventions came about.

CHAPTER TWO

The City and The Inventions

New York City in 1880 was far removed from the sophisticated and modern city of today.

The largest and most up-to-date city in the United States had no electric power, no lights, no telephones, no water system save for some houses having plumbing for cold water on the first or ground floor.

There were no bathrooms, no bridges either over the East River nor to New Jersey over the Hudson River.

Of course there was a limited means of personal communication primarily face to face, or in written long hand on paper.

E. B. noted that New York City's public transportation in the 1880's and 1890's was on horse drawn busses during the spring and summer months.

In the winter large open sleighs were used, with benches on either side and straw knee deep was used to keep the lower legs warm in the frigid temps.

The public transportation didn't venture north of 42nd Street. It was considered the hinterlands.

His early years recalled that shipping was all by sail and a transatlantic trip took two weeks by the fastest ships. Today it takes six hours or so by jet airplanes.

Even with the lack of facilities, E. B. recalled that there was plenty of food, plenty of clothing and excellent housing [especially for those of means]. Housing for immigrants and the lower classes was another story.

There were parts of New York where no member of the society class would venture. And according to E. B., it seemed as if there were jobs for those wanting to work, *"no organized labor, and no subversive elements!"*

He mentioned in his speech that industry was concentrated mostly in New York, Philadelphia and in the New England States.

Industry in those days consisted of small independent units taking real pride in their products, largely hand made, and selling them on a quality basis with no *"high pressure propaganda nor extravagant claims."*

He added, *"Life was ornamented by simple directness"*.

As a boy, his parents took him to see the fireworks marking the completion of the Brooklyn Bridge. The bridge, which took thirteen years to construct was completed in 1883. The event was attended by thousands of people and hundreds of boats sailed underneath in celebration. United States President Chester Arthur joined with New York Mayor Franklin Edison in the dedication. It is reported that more than 150,000 people followed the President and Mayor in a walk across the bridge on that grand day on May 24th.

The Brooklyn Bridge between Manhattan and Brooklyn, New York
[circa 1884]

After enrolling in the Stevens Institute at the young age of 17, E. B. built an electric motor, which ran but had very little power. He began to study gasoline-powered engines, which had recently been brought out by the Daimler Company in Germany [predecessor to Mercedes Benz].

He quickly developed a hydrocarbon engine in the Institute's machine shop, which was practically unknown in the U.S. at that time. He continued working on the development of gasoline-powered engines, which he thought, would bode well for him after graduation.

While a freshman at Stevens, the President of the Institute called him into his office one day.

The purpose was to introduce him to two executives of the Edison Light Company of New York.

The Edison Company had installed a lighting plant on 38th Street near 6th Avenue and Broadway in Manhattan and wanted to install one of their lights in a private home as an experiment.

E. B. was asked if he thought his parents would be willing to accept the offer. So without consulting them, E. B. agreed, and his home was the first in New York City to have one incandescent light in a private residence.

He recalled in his Newcomen speech that to accommodate the Edison supplied light, a China vase was used as the lamp. A hole was drilled in its bottom; he made a pedestal turned on a lathe at the Institute, plus a wood plug turned to fit into the neck. This then allowed it to receive the hand-made wire socket and to connect the wires.

His mother made a lace shade and visitors began to show up by the dozens to see this magical breakthrough in lighting up the dark evening hours.

The Edison Company didn't charge anything for the use, as there were no electric meters in those days. The current then had to be provided for free.

After two years of trial and error they finally developed a meter that was practical.

During the four years E. B. spent at The Stevens Institute, the high pressure water tube boiler was developed. This was made possible because steel became available which could withstand higher pressures.

Drs. Denton and Jacobs [Professors at The Stevens Institute] worked out a solution to the high-pressure steam boilers of Babcock and Wilcox, then the largest boiler company in the world.

Another inventor, Thomas Edison, was working on the phonograph while E. B. was still a student at The Institute. The principle of the phonograph, E. B. recalled, was possibly older than Edison's.

It was noted that one of his professors, Alfred M. Mayer, used to exhibit to his classes a phonograph having a cylinder with shallow grooves around its surface. On one end of the shaft was a handle and, as it was turned, the shaft carrying the cylinder moved horizontally in the bearings as it revolved.

A piece of tinfoil was wrapped carefully around and secured to the cylinder and a metal disc was mounted in a mouthpiece carrying a stylus resting on the tinfoil.

E. B. went on to describe the intricacies of this novel recording device with a hint of sarcasm in his writing, as noted in his Newcomen Society speech.

"To operate this contraption, one person would turn the handle at a uniform speed, while another would yell a message into the mouthpiece. Then the cylinder would be screwed back into its original position. The mouthpiece with its stylus placed against the cylinder was again cranked in its original direction. Using some imagination, you might recognize what you had yelled into the mouthpiece."

It is reported that Edison's device used wax instead of tin foil providing a regulated electrical drive. This was the start of an industry, which used the same principle for recording, dictation, music, and other records.

The evolving process eventually produced, many years later, such break through recording material and devices as vinyl records, eight track cassette tapes, cassettes, CDs, DVDs, mp3, digital recordings, and the evolution continues.

All of these new ways of sound recording and playback happened, of course, long after E. B.'s 1947 speech.

He noted for the record *"almost every important invention was anticipated by someone years before the real invention was made by the man who gave it to us in practical form."*

Continuing he said, *"Thus there were impractical incandescent lamps before Edison. Edison made them practical and rightfully is hailed as the inventor. There were steam carriages 120 years before he gasolene [sic] engine was developed, which in turn, made the automobile possible."*

Once the hot air engine was invented it created a demand for and began an industry of water pumps.

In New York City, tanks were built on top of buildings and water was driven from street-level pressure pumps into them. This allowed bathrooms and toilets to be made available on the second and third floor of houses. The newly pumped cold water then was made hot by simple gas heaters. This was the start of the plumbing industry in the United States.

E. B. recalled his family home in New York City was one of the first to have a bathroom installed with running hot and cold water. *"I remember scores of our friends calling and asking if they might see it!"* he noted.

His time spent at The Stevens Institute included some social as well as athletic endeavors. In 1892, President Hodgman of the Institute appointed E. B. to the "Junior Ball Committee." The dance was held shortly after Easter in 1893.

He also played center on the Varsity Football Team during his Junior and Senior Years. Although he indicated he wasn't the best of students, he did enjoy the extracurricular activities The Institute provided him.

The Stevens Institute Football Team 1893

E. B. football team is pictured above he is on the left side of the photo in the second row, wearing his signature mustache.

```
        1893  Middle States Football League (1-1-0)....

9/30   L 0-12     at Orange AC (at Orange Oval)
10/4   W 10-8        Crescent AC (H)
10/6   ??            NYAC (at Manhattan Field)
10/10  L 0-16     at Crescents (at Bay Ridge)
10/18  W 64-0        CCNY (H)
10/21  W 39-8     at Rutgers (Neilson Field) [First
                     League game]
10/25  L 10-12       Lafayette (H) [ League game]
```

E. B. Gallaher, Manager The Glee Club

He was a member of the Glee Club [singing bass], the Photography Club, the Engineering Club, the Mandolin Club, the Gun Club, manager of the Banjo Club, and a member of the fraternity Theta Nu Epsilon.

One may wonder if he had time for any thing resembling classes and studies during his college days. But he had a gift of perhaps a photographic memory, and an a determination to purse his interests aggressively.

> *"Commodore Phillips delivered the boat to me at Bayonne, New Jersey, where I had an engine made from my designs and installed. I then ran the boat about the bay [Hudson Bay] for several days to make sure it would work; next notified Commodore Phillips to come and get it."*

E. B. describing a gasoline engine he built and installed in a Schooner.

CHAPTER THREE

Graduation and Beyond

He continued the building of experimental electrical apparatus and hydrocarbon engines during his stay at Stevens, which left little time to study.

E. B. later recalled that he had been an indifferent student because of his work for the newspaper throughout his college career. Even with his varied interests, he appeared to be a mechanical genius.

The year was 1894 and Edward Beach Gallaher was handed his diploma as an official graduate of The Stevens Institute of Technology with a degree in Mechanical Engineering.

His diploma was unlike any others, as it was not only signed by the Institute's president, but also by its board of trustees and by every member of the faculty.

"*A present day [1940's] Stevens professor who saw it said he never had seen a diploma like it. Personally, I cannot yet see what induced all those scientists to risk their reputations,*" he commented.

Contributing to his resume was the fact that his thesis won first prize in the competition sponsored by the nationally distributed "Engineering News."

Shortly after his graduation at age 21, he set up an office and began looking for engineering work. He organized the Manhattan Manufacturing Company to make Maritime gasoline engines from his personal design.

Along the same lines, he organized another company called the Gallaher-Bayliss Engineering Company. This company would specialize in the construction of trolley roads and electric power plants.

He noted years later, *"Both concerns were quite successful."*

He recalled a story from his early engineering company years about a friend who was commodore of a yacht club.

It seemed the man owned a sizeable schooner-yacht called the *Southern Cross*. He inquired whether E. B. could design and install a gasoline engine in the launch, which was used to ferry passengers between the schooner and land. In its current state being very heavy it required four men rowing to move it in water.

"Commodore Phillips delivered the boat to me at Bayonne, New Jersey, where I had an engine made from my designs and installed. I then ran the boat about the bay [Hudson Bay] for several days to make sure it would work; next notified Commodore Phillips to come and get it," he said.

"Instead", he continued, *"he told me he would pay me the agreed price if he took delivery at Bayonne….that his yacht was lying in Flushing Harbor, and if I cared to run the launch across New York Bay, up the East River, through Hells Gate to Flushing, he would pay me one and a half times the agreed price."*

"I found out later he was afraid it would not run that long. At any rate, I made the trip from Bayonne to Flushing, delivered the launch, and earned a 50 percent bonus," he noted.

It was reported that Steinway, the piano manufacturer, had previously brought a Daimler gasoline powered launch from Germany. E. B. however claimed his was the first ever made in the U.S. The year was 1895 and E. B. was 22 years old.

It seems that about the same time, he became acquainted with the Johnson brothers of Cleveland, Ohio. They wanted to build trolley roads. E. B. became a consulting engineer for the next several years.

He was also devoting much of his efforts in designing a number of gas engine power plants for compressing air and for driving electric generators.

If not the youngest person he had to be close to it in the various engineering and mechanical organizations in which he was a member.

He was a member of the American Institute of Electrical Engineers, The American Society of Mechanical Engineers, and the New York Electrical Society. Not bad for a young man in his early twenties.

At the age of 22, E. B. was called upon to testify before the Mayor and Council of Auburn, New York. The subject was an extension of an electric railroad. E. B. had just completed testifying before the New York Rail Road Commission.

His thesis for The Stevens Institute was on the subject of electric power entitled "Test Of The Electric Railway Power Station At West Haven, Connecticut." This appears to be the reason he was ask to consult with the Auburn officials.

Among other things he told the folks at Auburn was very direct and to the point. He said their current rail road was the worst he had ever seen in his "experience" [again he was only a few years out of Stevens Institute].

As quoted in the Auburn Weekly Bulletin, May 23, 1895, he told the city fathers that *"a good road would change the city but a poor road would be a disgrace!"*

In 1896, just after turning 23, E. B. was contacted by John P. Holland who had just built a steam-powered submarine. The heat generated by the engine made it impractical for underwater use. He wondered E. B. could design a gasoline engine to replace the steam plant.

He did just that, he built a gasoline-powered marine engine for Holland, and it was considered the first ever to be used in an underwater craft. He called on his experience at The Institute and subsequent years of engine design to complete the request.

During this period of time a number of inventions took place. One in particular impressed E. B. and he told the story of another friend of the family one George Westinghouse. Mr. Westinghouse had invented a new airbrake for the railroads and was struggling to get it adopted by the carriers.

"He then turned his attention to electricity, working at first, along the same lines as Edison in the production of direct current apparatus" E. B. recalled. Westinghouse and Edison had a feud over whether electric current should be, "AC or DC?"

"One day, Nicola Tesla described to Mr. Westinghouse his invention made in 1887 of the polyphrase alternating-current motor and generator, which made the use of alternating current practical."

"This marked the beginning of the giant development of high-tension electric transmission, in which the Westinghouse Company played a major role.

Another invention of the period had to do with ship propulsion. He recalled that before 1880 sailing ships had power from using auxiliary steam engines.

From 1880 on, and with the advances in boiler pressures, they had increased dramatically. This was the force behind the propulsion.

In his Newcomen Society speech, E. B. rattled off the following numbers:

"In 1855 boiler pressures rose from 10 to 20 lbs. In 1865 the screw propeller began to displace the paddle wheel, and the boiler pressures rose from 20 lbs. to 35 lbs.

"In 1875, the compound engine began to replace the simple engine, and boiler pressure rose from 35 lbs. to 60 lbs."

"In 1885, steel replaced iron in the hull construction, the triple expansion engine came in, and boiler pressures rose from 60 lbs. to 125 lbs."

"In 1895, we find quadruple-expansion engines with steam pressure of 200 lbs."

"During this evolutionary process, fuel consumption dropped from 4.5 to 1.3 lbs per horsepower."

It seems as if E. B. was taken with the progress of containing steam pressure even though he moved toward developing the gasoline engine as time went by.

Besides Westinghouse E. B. had been personally befriended by Thomas Edison, J.P. Morgan, Charles Schwab [before the brokerage house was even thought of] Andrew Carnegie, John Wanamaker, E. H. Harriman, John Jacob Astor, among other leading industrialists and bankers of the time.

E. B. driving his Keystone Motorette in Philadelphia.

CHAPTER FOUR

An Original "Car Guy"

In between these ventures, he also tinkered with designs for a "horseless carriage" and did so before reaching the age of 23. A year later he built his first car the "Keystone Motorette," and unveiled it in Philadelphia.

This was the beginning of his automobile manufacturing, and in 1897 his company sold several units.

E. B. recalled that the first cars had a single-cylinder 2.5 horsepower gasoline engine, tethered to a tubular frame with bicycle wheels and tires. The car had one speed both forward and reverse. The motor was under the rear seat and the car was steered by a lever. Top speed on a smooth road…..5 m.p.h.

He obtained financing and rented an abandoned factory in Philadelphia and adopted the name "Keystone Motor Company."

His idea was to build a car for the masses at a cost of about $500. He remarked later, *"The idea was good, but I was a few years too soon!"*

Sales were mediocre at best until a stroke of luck befell him. It involved his competitive nature and a desire to win, whatever the activity or challenge.

Whenever the opportunity arose, he would make the most of it in an effort to promote his new product.

He befriended two customers who drove the Schuylkill Road every day at a speed of five miles per hour until they reached an area with a long down hill.

Going down this hill, the car reached 10 miles per hour and the momentum would carry them up the other side going up about 100 yards.

The brakes were not the best going forward and non-existent going backwards, so when the car stalled, out jumped E. B. and he put a wedge rock behind the wheel to avoid going backwards.

He noted that every so often a man who looked like Santa Claus, driving a horse drawn carriage would race by them, laughing at their lack of power.

It seems as if the "horseless carriage" was being out run by the "horse drawn carriage" and by a wide margin.

Not to be denied, E. B. tried to figure a way to get a "leg up" on the speed game so he used his promotion skills to lay out a plan of action.

In the Newcomen Society speech, he told the following story.

"One day I read in the paper that the city fathers had passed an ordinance limiting the speed of horseless carriages to five miles per hour," he noted.

"The next day I was out as usual; bowled along the drive at five miles per hour…..down the grade at ten miles per hour….up City Line Hill to a stop, where I had just chocked my wheels, when an officer appeared and asked me if I did not know that a new five-mile ordinance had been passed.

My mind worked quickly in those days….I asked the officer how fast I was going; he said he had timed me at ten miles per hour. I then asked him where I was and he told me to quit kidding….I knew I was going up City Line Hill. I then said, 'Will you tell the Court that you arrested me going up City Line Hill?' He said he would and I gave him a bill."

E. B. then went back to the office and notified all the newspapers that the first arrest for speeding would be tried in court the next day. They all showed up for the hearing.

"We were waiting for the Judge to come in when who should appear but my friend, Santa Claus, with his long whiskers….he was the Judge. He asked for a copy of the ordinance; asked who was the defendant; and who made the arrest." he said.

"Then he inquired where the arrest was made and the officer said, 'Going up City Line Hill.' He then asked if he had timed me, and the officer admitted he had; then he asked how fast I was going, and the officer said: "Ten miles an hour your Honor."

"This was enough," E. B. recounted. *"The Judge said: Let me understand this correctly. You arrested this man going up City Line Hill at ten miles an hour…..is that correct?   The officer said, 'Yes'.   Then came: "Impossible….case dismissed."*

The notoriety of this "set up" news story attracted attention of some Philadelphia well-heeled gentlemen, according to E. B.   Among them were some of the top business leaders in Philadelphia where E. B. had set shop a few years earlier. It wasn't long before he pulled together a few of the Philadelphia elate.

44

"In the latter part of 1900 a number of important men were brought together to form a company to take over my Keystone Motor Company. Two of them were Theodore C. Search, head of the Stetson Hat Works, and Charles H. Graham, referred to in those days as "The Silver King."

E. B. noted that the name of the company was changed to incorporate Mr. Search's financial participation. Thus the "Searchmont" Motor Company was inaugurated in October, 1900.

The manufacturing of the small car under the Searchmont moniker called for the expansion of operations. The cars were then made available for sale first by the Wanamaker Stores in Philadelphia and New York.

Wikipedia noted that Keystone Waggonette, now called The Searchmont was a Runabout for two passengers with a water cooled single cylinder engine in a compartment under the seat and had a chain drive. It stayed in production until 1902 and the later version cost $750.

The other partner Graham, was described by E. B. as *"an 'elegant type', considerably over six feet tall, straight as an arrow...always wore a frock coat and silk hat, a velvet stock, and carried a gold-headed ebony cane."*

"Mr. Graham called me one day and said he would like to ride in one of our horseless carriages; and made a date to meet me on Broad Street. At the appointed hour he drove up in a magnificent coach with a coachman and footman. He then got into my little car and sat beside me....his knees almost touched his chin, and he sat with his cane grasped between his legs....his tall stovepipe hat towering over me. I asked where he would like me to take him, and he said: 'Let's drive down Broad Street to the financial district."

"As we approached the financial district, people were clearing a path for us because they could hear us coming for a half mile; when all of a sudden Mr. Graham lost his nerve and asked me to pull up to the curb. That ended the trip, but I felt in my bones that something was coming."

"At the next board meeting, Mr. Graham told of his ride...stated that he did not believe there were enough people in the county who would be willing to pay $500 for a horseless carriage; then said he would propose to the Board that we abandon the manufacture of this cheap vehicle and design a new and larger car that a gentleman could ride in and not be come embarrassed. That settled it."

E. B. noted that the Board instructed him to complete the cars under construction, and meanwhile design a new and larger car, which he did.

As a side note to the Searchmont story, E. B. said that the car had a starter operated by a foot pedal. A spark plug was developed, identical to those made fifty years later, but not as reliable. So the cars were equipped with both sparkplugs and contact ignition systems so if one did not worked the other was available.

Over the years A. C. Spark Plug Company [part of General Motors] in Flint, Michigan produced millions of "spark" plugs for cars all over the world. [The "A.C." stood for Albert Champion, the inventor of spark plugs].

There were no gas stations in those days so gasoline had to be secured from paint and hardware stores.

The vendors sold it for cleaning purposes and for home lighting. The gas wasn't much better than kerosene and some of it used for home lighting was very volatile.

E. B. wrote, *"The challenge was that one never knew what type of gas was going to be available and only one grade of gasoline would work with the carburetor. It was necessary to adjust our 'gas' and 'air' every time we put new gas in our tank….this was done from the dashboard and became one of our major problems."*

One of the major challenges to manufacturing automobiles in the turn of the Century was there was no equipment available to build the 'horseless carriage."

Everything at Searchmont Motor Car and other car manufacturers at the time had to be built in their own shops. Designs had to be made for Chassis, axles, engines, spark plugs, springs, wheels, body, upholstery, etc.

Because the call was for a larger and heavier car, the former wheels and tires from bicycles could no longer be used.

The first tires tried were made from rope cured in hot asphaltum. The three-inch rope with a long splice was reportedly "hard riding!"

One day in early 1901, E. B. made a call on the Diamond Rubber Tire store on Cortland Street in New York City. He inquired if a larger tire could be made for his motorcar company. Reportedly the representative said no….but one of the company executives, W. B. Miller overheard the conversation from the back of the offices and came out.

Clincher tire with inner tube for E. B.'s later automobiles.

"I told Mr. Miller what I wanted, and without hesitation he said 'We'll make it for you'. He then accompanied me back to Philadelphia to see what we required; and made up special molds for a 3" heavy tread single-tube tire."

Continuing E. B. noted, *"Mr. Miller and his chief engineer came to our plant later with a set of these tires, which they put on the car themselves....while on jacks....but when we lowered it to the floor, the rims touched the ground.*

Mr. Miller made new molds three times, before he produced a tire which supported the load."

"I cannot say whether these were the first strictly automobile tires or not, but they certainly were among the first. This was several years before the clincher tire with an inner tube made its appearance, and was the beginning of our great tire industry," he concluded.

Reportedly, with this breakthrough, E. B. made the first trip in one of his manufactured "horseless carriages" from Philadelphia to New York; and from Philadelphia to Baltimore and Washington D. C.

He always brought two cars on these adventures in an attempt to establish a driving record. One car to establish the record, and a second loaded with spare parts and a few mechanics!

Commenting on his experiences during these record-breaking attempts, E. B. noted that many interesting things happened.

"One of the funniest was when we passed through Shaking-Quaker country, it was at a time when they were harvesting their grain crops. I remember every time we would meet a four-horse reaper and binder, the horses would take fright and dash away over the hills with the driver in pursuit. They must have loved us!"

E. B. also recalled winning an award in Philadelphia from the Cycle Board of Trade at its annual bicycle exhibition. Searchmont Car Company was invited to exhibit a car....and the Board of Trade changed the name to add "car" to the show title.

"We were awarded a beautiful bronze medal with an engraving of our 'Waggonette' and on the back 'For the best designed Automobile in the Show'…..which was most natural as ours was the only automobile in the exhibit," he said.

The Searchmont Motor Company underwent another name change to incorporate the racecar driver named Henri Furnier to take advantage of the publicity and advertising inherent with his participation. Furnier became the company's driver for car races. It was a stroke of genius as it helped position the new car company as a most competitive operation.

Furnier began his racing career in motorcycles and in 1901 he joined the Mors Racing Team [an early French car manufacturer] and won two major European races, the Paris to Bordeaux and the Paris to Berlin events.

Furnier also set a record in America for the fastest mile by a race car, and later set the then land speed record at 123 km/h. [a bit over 73 miles per hour].

However, the Frenchman wasn't the only driver for the company, as E. B. recounted in his Newcomen Society speech. He said he still had the newspaper clipping dated Jamaica, Long Island, April 26, 1902. The other driver was E. B. himself.

A Keystone Waggonette [circa 1902]

"The greatest assembly of automobiles up to this date in this country......there were 80 cars entered in the race. All cars mentioned in the article were of foreign manufacture with a single exception of one American Searchmont driven my me," he said.

At least one of the early Searchmont Cars survived over the years, because in 2006 at Pebble Beach in California, one sold at auction for $132,000.

Dan Vaughn of Conceptcarz.com [a terrific car guy website] wrote about it in a column on his site.

"Theodore Search of the Stetson Hat Company and Spencer Trask purchased the Keystone Motor Company of Philadelphia in 1900. The result of that buyout was the Searchmont Motor Company. Search and Trask had seen potential with the evolving automobile and with the Keystone Motor Company.

Keystone had been creating single-cylinder, rear engine runabouts and delivery wagons that had been done with much success. Their vehicles were lightweight and the five-cylinder engine was suitable to carry the vehicles along at a modest pace. With the buyout, the Searchmont retained the services of Keystone's plant manager, Edward. B. Gallagher [sic].

For the first two years of the Searchmont existence, the vehicles produced mimicked the styling of their predecessors. Little was changed until Frenchman Henri Fournier came aboard.

Fournier had gained a reputation as a racing driver and was given the task of creating a new design for the Searchmont automobiles.

The result of his work was not seen until 1903. His contributions to the Searchmont automobile included the use of force-feed lubrication, which made it the first of its kind in the U.S.

Lee S. Chadwick aided Fournier in the design and engineering of the new vehicles. Soon, the duo had created a powerful, 32-horsepower four-cylinder engine that helped Searchmont outpace their competition.

The price tag for a Searchmont quickly escalated, costing twice as much as other marques such as Ford or Cadillac. The demand for this price was due to the vehicles reliability, style, and advanced engineering.

Sadly, their place in history was short lived. Trask, who had been a big financial backer of the company, lost a large amount of money in the stock market and was forced to rescind his support to the company.

The sales of the cars began to dwindle, and when the company finally did close its doors, was still left with inventory which included about 100 examples of the two-cylinder car.

The companies remaining inventory was purchased by John Wanamaker for $750 each, which was a heavily reduced price and a bargain for Wanamaker.

Wanamaker was in the business of department stores and used his stores for the sale of his line of automobiles. The cars were sold at a price of $1250 per vehicle, which was still a bargain for both buyer and seller.

This 1904 Searchmont Touring automobile is a rear-entranced vehicle that is powered by a two-cylinder engine that produces an adequate 10 horsepower. The engine uses a double-chain drive to turn the wheels and features the force-feed engine lubrication system.

The gorgeous body sits atop an 81-inch wheelbase and is believed to be the only Searchmont in existence. It has wonderful, period correct, brass accents, wicker tonneau baskets, and leather upholstery.

It has received a national first place award from the Antique Automobile Club of America and is eligible for the London-to-Brighton event.   It was offered for sale at the 2006 Gooding & Company Auction in Pebble Beach where it was estimated to sell between $80,000-$110,000. There was much interest in this car during auction day, as automotive enthusiasts opened their hearts and their wallets to drive the price up to an impressive $132,000.

Dan Vaughn Conceptcarz.com

1904 Searchmont Touring Automobile

Charles Schwab comments to E. B.

E. B.'s commentary on Mr. Schwab's shortsightedness.

CHAPTER FIVE

"Pre" Grand Prix

One of the challenges faced by those interested in manufacturing was the poor quality of steel. Parts that required strength such as springs, shafts, and axles kept breaking.

E. B. noted that the French and Germans in building their early cars didn't breakdown as much as his were doing.

As previously noted, the car produced by Furnier drove from Paris to Berlin and at a reportedly good rate of speed with no breakdowns.

Learning of this feat, E. B. went to Europe and contacted two manufacturers, one in Paris and the other in Stuttgart.

As a result of these contacts E. B. became a consultant to both the Richard-Brasier Works and the Daimler Works.

The French car company was designing a car to compete in the French eliminations for the Gordon Bennett Cup Race. E. B. said he had worked on the car and learned their secret.

The car eventually won the races and when the prize money was distributed E. B. reported that he saw over one-half go to a small, but very old steel manufacturer, called Lemoin.

This company for many generations had been working on the fine carriage forgings and hardware for the great coach-builders in England and in Europe. They also supplied a company in New York called Brewster.

E. B. told the story of visiting the plant and found a few hundred men making alloy steels in 100 lb. billets. The steel had two to three times the strength of the steel available in America and it could be tempered.

All the foreign car manufacturers were getting alloy steel from this company so the springs found on their cars, along with axles, gears, drive shafts and the like would withstand the stress.

E. B. said then he arranged to have the same alloy steel sent to America for use in the Philadelphia plant.

The "Gordon Bennett Cup Race" was changed to the "Grand Prix" the following year and the Brasier cars won two successive years, winning six times overall.

The strategy of the Brasier car company when it came to racing according to E. B. was to constantly seek improvements in the development of the car. Each year as they won, they would again give Lemoin some of the prize money and tell the owner to begin working for the next year.

The company proposed to reduce the weight of the car by 25 per cent and increase the power by the same percentage.

On the ocean liner return trip from Europe to New York, E. B. happened to have his deck chair next to Charles Schwab who at that time was a great steel manufacturer.

The story of the Lemoin and Brasier connection was shared with him and E. B. noted that he asked Schwab to do the same...make alloy steel.

Schwab responded that his company could make any kind of steel as long as there was a demand and the order would have to be for 1000 tons.

E. B. is reported to have indicated that an amount equal to the Schwab's basic order would last them ten years. He asked Schwab couldn't it be made like Lemoin did it, in 100 lb. billets?   At this point, E. B. recounts what happened next.

He said that Schwab then turned to him and said, *"Gallaher, you are wasting your life over these horseless carriages, they will never amount to anything!"*

"It shows how even a brilliant man sometimes could be mistaken if lacking sufficient vision." E. B. wrote.

That wasn't the end of the story however, as time went by E. B. learned of an newspaper article in New York City, which indicated that the prospect of making this type of steel in America had arrived.

It took some time for the idea to come to fruition, but E. B. tells the following story of what happened to change Schwab's mind.

"Mr. Schwab had a change of heart, because some years later in an interview reported in the New York World in 1906, he said: 'While in Germany this summer I saw them making automobile parts of the same fine steel used in guns.'

"Now, how can our products compete with that sort of thing? When I returned from Germany, not so many weeks ago, I had a large shop for making high-grade forged automobile parts set up beside the Bethlehem Steel Work. We have already received orders for the full capacity of the shop for a year ahead."

E. B. developed a passion for racing, partly as a promotion vehicle to sell cars. A blurb in the Stevens Institute Newsletter recalled an incident in which E. B. won a race but was disqualified for going too fast!

"E. B. Gallaher, general manager of the Fournier-Searchmont Automobile Co. of Philadelphia, entered three of his Searchmont cars in the Long Island 100 mile endurance run last April. All three cars were disqualified for having completed the course at faster rate than 15 miles per hour. There seems to have been some misunderstanding in general about the maximum allowable rate, and Mr. Gallaher presents a strong letter in The Horseless Age of April 30 against the injustice of the disqualification."

Not to be outdone by rules he judged to be arbitrary, E. B. seemed to be fuming at the disqualification for "speeding" in a car race.

Even The New York Times picked up on the controversy when the following appeared:

November 1, 1903
The New York Times

"At the close of the day's racing the win of E. B. Gallaher's car was protested, as his car did not come within the conditions and the judges gave a profisional disqulificagtion. [sic]

The Results:

Five Miles: For stock cars of any motive power weighing under 1,200 pounds.

Class B – First prize, silver trophy, value $100 – Won by Edward. B. Gallaher's 16 h.p. Georges Richard Brazier gasoline car.

He also won his heat race in the Five Mile, Handicap Gentlemen Operators; [cars operated by owners], but lost the Final Heat Race.

E. B. sensed that the future
be one in which the masses would r
automobiles for transportation.

He recalled the story of one of the
Automobile Club members in New York
City who happened to be standing near a
window suggesting that they count how
many automobiles might pass by in an
hour.

Notable was the fact that assembled
in that room was the Club President Albert
R. Shattuck, a past President, Winthrop E.
Scarrit; plus members David H. Morris,
John Jacob Astor, and an English Lord
whose name E. B. couldn't remember.

After counting four in an hour they
were so impressed they went over to the
Club register, entered the startling fact,
stated in their collective belief that the
automobile was here to stay! All of them
signed the statement. It must have been
cocktail hour at the Club.

By 1905 the automobile was on its
way to becoming an accepted mode of
transportation, even still in its infancy.

Touring car built by Searchmont Motor Co. in Philadelphia, Pa in the center [E. B. is believed to be the man climbing into the car]. This was taken during the New York to Buffalo endurance run September 9-13, 1901. **The Searchmont was entered by E.B. Gallaher and the entry # is B-51, 52, or 53.** [Courtesy of the National Automotive History Collection, Detroit Public Library]

The simultaneous development in Europe and the U. S. of the gasoline engine was the catalyst for progress made in the manufacturing of the "horseless carriage".

E. B. was an original if not founding member of the American Automobile Association with Headquarters on Fifth Avenue in New York City.

He also was chairman of the organization's Technical Committee, which oversaw the AAA's racing program.

E. B. never claimed to be the first who made a gasoline engine powered vehicle, as there were several made a year or two before his vehicles.

His first vehicle was in operation in 1896 and in production in 1897.

Several hundred of the small cars were made between that year and 1900 under the name of Keystone Motor Company. As noted earlier, it was then absorbed by the Searchmont Motor Company, which increased production and redesigned the model.

The AAA had numerous social events as well as sponsoring races. One of the outings was written up in the New York Times.

Unique Automobile Trip.

A unique automobiling entertainment entitled "A Holiday Trip Around the World in an Automobile" will be held under the direction of Winthrop E. Scarrett, Vice President of the Automobile Club of America, at East Orange, N. J., on the afternoon and evening of May 30. The plan is to have various prominent houses decorated to represent the different countries to be visited. Some of the finest motor cars in America will be in service. They will start from a central station, carrying the tourists first to Berlin, Germany, represented by the home of W. R. Wilson on Maple Street. Thence the travellers journey to Paris, France, home of Mr. and Mrs. Searles, Arlington Avenue. From the French capital they will go on to the fascinating land of the "Rising Sun," Japan, represented by the residence of Winthrop E. Scarritt, 44 Munn Avenue. Here will be found beautiful Japanese maidens serving tea in Tokio, and selling wonderfully artistic souvenirs of this quaint people. From the Japanese capital a journey by easy stages will be made to London, the home of G. F. Park, on Walnut Street, and thence back to East Orange, where the weary traveler will find abundant refreshment.

The motor cars will be decorated with flowers and flags. Among the more prominent cars will be H. W. Whipple's fine "Mercedes," C. M. Mabley's "Panhard," E. B. Gallaher's "Vivinus," T. M. Hilliard's "Panhard," and John A. Hill's "Pan-American."

He also held a number of positions in a variety of companies. One of which he reported to his alma mater in 1903: *"E. B. Gallaher ('94) is general manager of the Mobile Company of America, Broadway and 54th Street, New York, NY."*

It seems he left that post after a short time, as the "Cycle and Automotive Trade Journal" reported the company had a new manager by the name of J. C. Walker in its July 1, 1903 issue.

E. B. started the Clover Manufacturing Company in 1903 in New York City at the age of 30.

He continued his interest in automobiles however, taking trips back and forth to Europe during the early part of the 20th Century.

Besides his consulting with French and German car manufacturers, E. B. was looking for another way to promote the "Richard-Brasier" cars even with the idea to bring the famous race car driver Leon Thery to New York. Thery won the most famous race in Europe two years in a row.

New York Times
September 17. 1905

AUTO TOURISTS RETURN.

W. E. Scarritt Sees Greater Possibilities for Motor Cars In the Future.

Winthrop E. Scarritt returned yesterday from Europe on the steamer La Touraine. He has been enjoying an automobile trip through France with J. H. Hill and C. H. Kavenaugh. Mr. Scarritt said he had a delightful journey through the most picturesque parts of Switzerland and France.

"The present tour," he added, "has broadened my horizon regarding the possibilites of the automobile as one of the vital forces in the progress of civilization."

On the same steamer was E. B. Gallaher, the American agent for the Richard-Brasier cars. Mr. Gallaher went abroad hoping to make arrangements to bring over the winning Gordon Bennett car and its driver, Thery. The latter, however, decided he had done enough road racing, and having made considerable money from his past victories, has virtually retired from speed contests. The two Richard-Brasier cars, therefore, that had been picked for the French team, withdrew. Mr. Gallaher said he had strong hopes of a French team victory, and stated that the Vanderbilt race was attracting considerable attention from foreign automobilists.

His interest in automobiles was unabated and he road the crest of popularity with the advances made each year in the new automobile industry.

A new Brasier car will be shown in a few days, by E. B. Gallaher. It is rated at 40-50 horse power, and has a direct drive on the third and fourth speeds, a new type of selective transmission, a new carbureter, and a new clutch. There is also a novel arrangement of two fans, one in the position of an ordinary fan, behind the radiator and an exhaust fan in the flywheel. It will be ready for demonstrating purposes within a few days.

In a letter to the editor of <u>The Automobile</u> <u>magazine</u> E. B. was not hesitant to share his displeasure with an article reportedly damaging the reputation of his current automobile import business.

April, 1907
The Automobile

"It is all very well to damn the French car, and state how fine the American car is, and there is no question that a good many of the American cars are really good, but is absolutely wrong in my estimation, to steal any man's thunder and to take one of the best machines in the world and try to build up the reputation of an American machine on the already made reputation of a high-class foreign car. I kept still during the last campaign of free advertising on the Brasier reputation, but I do not propose at the present time to keep quiet any longer."

An article in <u>The New York Times</u> five years later in 1908 noted he solved a problem facing mechanics at the time.

> A problem with the repair man who tackles valve grinding has always been the securing of a compound which will not stiffen up and become too thick after standing a while. This difficulty is now overcome by the Clover valve grinding compound, which is put out by the Clover Manufacturing Company at 230 West Fifty-eighth Street.

His Clover Manufacturing was in full swing by this time, and E. B. did his best to promote it. But he also used advertisements to promote his business interests.

MODEL F. 30-35 H. P.
CLEVELAND PHAETON DOUBLE TULIP. $3,500.
COMPLETELY GUARANTEED FOR ONE YEAR.
Exhibit at 69th Regiment Armory.

E. B. Gallaher, 228-230 W. 58th St., N. Y.
Paris Office, No. 11 Rue d'Alger.

Sole Importer.
RICHARD-BRASIER.

General Eastern Distributer.
CLEVELAND MOTOR CAR CO.

He took a number of trips back and forth between New York and the Continent on various ocean liners during this time as his passport records.

It seems as if E. B. had a knack of getting mentioned in the <u>Times</u> for another article appeared on March 8, 1908.

E. B. Gallagher, manager of the American branch of the Maja Company, will give the Bostonians a chance to see the new Maja car. He will drive from New York to Boston tomorrow, and, beginning Tuesday, will give demonstrations in Boston. This is done because of repeated requests on the part of the New England people to see the Maja. One of the forty-five horse power touring cars will be used.

The Maja Company, Limited, of England, has obtained control of the body building plant heretofore known as Sayers & Co., at 90 Wandsworth Road, Vauxhall, London, and will in future use this shop exclusively for the building of bodies for Maja cars. Sayers & Co. have long been among the foremost body builders of England, their work challenging comparison with the products of the best Italian, German, and French experts. The plant consists of about twenty departments covering the production and finishing of almost every style of body. About 500 workmen are employed.

E. B. continued to get good news coverage as indicated by the following New York Times article of June 7, 1908:

TRADE CONDITIONS ABROAD.

Foreign Makers Interested In Conditions In This Country.

E. B. Gallaher, Manager of the Majas, American branch, has just returned from Europe. He says that most of the French and German makers of cars are looking to America for a market with wistful eyes. Trade conditions abroad are not what they have been during the last two years, and as a result the foreigners have begun to figure on America in a way they have never before figured. " Price fluctuations are the order of the day," he says, "and the sudden interest of the foreign clubs in the Automobile Club's Grand Prize, run under international rules, may be interpreted as indicating the instinct toward a European invasion. I look for an unusual increase in motor car imports."

And this announcement was made about E. B.'s connection with another publication for the early motoring public in Europe and beyond, as published a few months later.

The New York Times
August 30, 1908

The Motor Union's Handbook.

The Motor Union of Great Britain has just published a foreign handbook, which has been compiled with the object of facilitating Continental touring and enabling members of the union to reach their desired destination with the least possible trouble. This book includes the full customs and road regulations of all European countries, of Egypt, and of Asiatic Turkey. It also gives considerable information on these points as to America, Australia, South Africa, India, China, and Japan.

E. B. Gallaher, who is the American representative of the Motor Union, states that it is the most exhaustive book of its kind which he has ever seen. In the complete list of hotels given the approximate cost of meal and sleeping accommodations is separately itemized. In the 200 pages there is a mass of useful information.

E. B. had a talent for identifying automobiles which would be popular with the upper echelon driving public. Most models were out of the reach of the vast majority of Americans. It seems as if the total number of cars on the road during this time was under 10,000.

The average wage in 1907 was 22 cents per hour and the annual income was between $200 to $400 for the average American. But the most challenging thing for car salesmen was that there was only 144 miles of paved roads in those days.

His evolution from building engines to designing and developing gas powered cars to automobile racing to importer of foreign cars to creator of motoring guidebooks put E. B. in circles of economic and social influence.

> *"Our brains and our energies first were concentrated upon the conception and development of these basic inventions....and then upon their grouping to form huge industries. Today we find ourselves with enormous industrial strength...great laboratories, thousands of skilled technicians, only to be confronted by a new and radical change in our economic condition."*

E. B. commenting on the progress of inventions.

CHAPTER SIX

Inventions and More

In his 1947 Newcomen Society speech, E. B. pointed out that people in their 70's, as he was, have had the opportunity for intimate knowledge of and in many cases the opportunity to take part in creating "more inventions and more developments" than probably any others ever have seen and known.

During his lifetime he took out several patents many relating to the automobile field. Some of them were still in use by the late 1940's and beyond. The invention described below is one of many reflecting the creative mind and practical applications.

"PATENT FOR A "ROLL DESPENSING DEVICE"

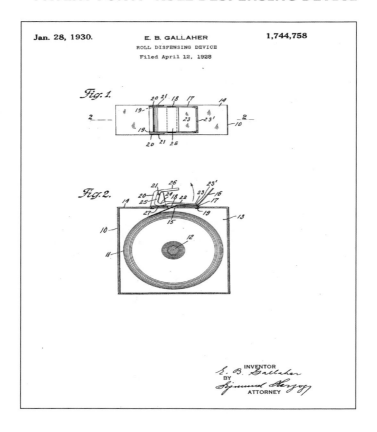

Jan. 28, 1930.   E. B. GALLAHER   1,744,758
ROLL DISPENSING DEVICE
Filed April 12, 1928

"*It should be appreciated that from 1880 to 1905 most of our great basic inventions were made, and that manufacturing companies were engaged in building the foundation upon which rests our present day development,*" he said.

Among the practical commercially relevant inventions in the 1880's - 1900's recounted in his speech were the following:

- Airbrake
- Airplane
- Alloy steels
- Alternating current

- Artificial abrasives
- Arc light
- Automatic car coupler
- Automobile

- Bessemer steel
- Bicycle
- Cream separator
- Cyanide steel-making process

- Cylinder printing press
- Diesel engine
- Dry plate and photographic film
- Electric welding

- Electric generator
- Elevator
- Gasoline engine
- Gramophone

- Harvey steel-hardening process
- High-frequency dynamo and motor
- High temperature electric furnace
- High-tension electric transmission

- Incandescent lamp
- Internal combustion engine
- Linotype
- Marconi wireless

- Motion pictures
- Phonograph
- Producer gas
- Pneumatic tire

- Reaper and binder
- Screw propeller
- Sewing machine
- Silicon Carbide and Aluminum Oxide

- Smokeless powder
- Steam turbine
- Storage batteries
- Telegraph
- Telephone

- Tractor
- Trolley car
- Typewriter
- Vulcanization of rubber
- Zinc plate etching and halftone process

He noted that every one of these inventions formed the base of some great enterprise and gave employment to millions of workers and at the same time increased the standard of living to heights unimaginable 50 years earlier.

"Our brains and our energies first were concentrated upon the conception and development of these basic inventions….and then upon their grouping to form huge industries. Today we find ourselves with enormous industrial strength…great laboratories, thousands of skilled technicians, only to be confronted by a new and radical change in our economic condition," he stated.

An invention from 1909, which was patented as an "improved coin-handling device" [patent application number 21,744] seemed to be an odd interest of E. B., since most of his other patents were related to the automobile and manufacturing systems.

> ANY American motorist is welcome to our services and our best efforts no matter what car he may own or prefer—his automobile creed does not enter into the question. He is an American motorist about to tour abroad, and hence we are at his service, not only here, but abroad, and on his arrival and departure.

Excerpt from an ad E. B. placed in a newspaper.

CHAPTER SEVEN

The Talents of E. B.

E. B. continued to innovate and take advantage of his mechanical genius. Up until this time he was the importer of the Brasier Automobile from France and made frequent trips to France during this time.

He started an "auto service" in Paris, basically to help foreigners, mostly Americans, navigate the terrain in France and the rest of Europe.

E. B. in his travels to Europe used his automobile knowledge and expertise to further broaden his business portfolio.

He used his contacts on the Continent to his advantage and was able to secure a foothold in the burgeoning import-export business of the day.

One of his many trips was written up in <u>The Times</u> and is described as follows:

The New York Times
November 23, 1904

Automobilists Sail For Big Paris Show

Clarence Gray Dinsmore, the newly elected Third Vice President of the Automobile Club of America, sailed for Europe yesterday on the Kaiser Wilhelm der Grosse, which carried a large party of automobilists, many of whom are going over to attend the Paris automobile salon, which opens Dec. 8.........

.........Among the importers of foreign cars who sailed for the purpose of studying new French models as they will be exhibited at the coming show in Paris, and to arrange to bring some of the latest cars from France to this city for the big show in January, were E. B. Gallaher, Frank Eveland, Sidney B. Bowman, E. R. Thomas, Harold Pope, and H. A. Linehart.

> *Mr. Gallaher, before sailing, stated that he had just received information that the Gordon Bennett car which Thery will drive in the coming race has been completed and will have a road test within a short time. This car is of the same general type as the one used by Thery last season when he won the race and took the cup back to France.*

Another reference to E. B. and his ventures in Europe is described in "Three Men In A Motor Car" a book written in 1906 by Winthrop E. Scarritt.

E. B. and Scarritt shared an interest in automobiles and in racing, traveling, and later in politics. However Scarritt once said he would leave the country if it didn't support Theodore Roosevelt. E. B. as it turns out later was one of those that was totally against the politics of another Roosevelt.....Franklin Delano.

Scarritt was endeavoring to drive through France and visit various cities, but ran into trouble along the way. He describes his adventures as follows:

> *".....after arriving in Paris, I met that human dynamo of enterprise and energy, E. B. Gallaher. I described to him the troubles we had experienced in getting started out of Harve — the utter impossibility of getting the Frenchmen to move quickly.*

I told him in emphatic language what I thought of foreign officials as a class, and ended by stating that when a man was dead, and knew he was dead there was still some hope for him, but the foreign officials were dead and didn't know it, and here was really the foundation of all our troubles.

Mr. Gallaher listened patiently to my tale of trouble and then informed me that he had come to Paris to solve these vexatious problems confronting American tourists.

I found that he had established an extensive bureau at No. 11 Rue D'Alger where the American automobile tourist could come and be put right.

I discovered that this gentleman had been spending a goodly portion of his time the past few years in helping fellow members of the Automobile Club in particular, and Americans in general, in getting straightened out when they go into trouble in the French capital, and finally, such was the increasing demand for such services, he had decided to establish a European headquarters in Paris, with branches in London and Stuttgart.

This he has done, and he is prepared to do absolutely everything for the automobilist that is now being done for the ordinary tourist by the great express companies and the tourist companies, viz -- shipping their cars from America to any point in Europe, supplying chauffeurs, obtaining licenses and insurance, looking after repairs and spare parts, and, where designed even supplying both car and man to meet parties anywhere in England or on the continent.

> *My satisfaction at hearing all this can only be measured by the thought of what our party would have escaped had we known of my friend Gallaher's scheme before leaving America. The idea of being able to turn over our worry, annoyance, and expense to someone who would attend to it all made me feel that I would like to start right out again, if only for the pleasure of seeing someone else do what we, only a few weeks ago, had looked upon as he impossible – make the Frenchman hustle.*
>
> *I should state that this bureau is the first and only thing of the kind in existence and it certainly fills a great need. Mr. Gallaher has had the good judgment today this new department out on the broadest lines. Any American is welcome to its services. No matter what car a man may own or prefer -- his automobile creed does not enter into the question. If the traveler is an American, that is sufficient."*

Scarritt later became President of the American Automobile Club and died in 1912.

E. B. expanded his business interests to include shipping cars from the U.S. to Europe, chauffeurs for those not wanting to drive on "foreign" roads, as well as car rentals for those that might want to tour on their own [plus maps!].

Even though he had a knack at getting free publicity in the City's newspapers, on occasion he would take advertisements out to publicize his business ventures.

One of his latest automobile related activities was illustrated in a 1907 ad.

E. B. honed his writing ability during this time, as he would regularly send notices to the various newspapers in New York City. It seemed as if he was his own press agent.

Once his motoring guides were established, he promoted his travel consultancy as reported in The New York Times:

> ### The New York Times
> ### May 12, 1908
>
> E. B. Gallaher of the Maja Company reports an unprecedented demand for the European touring itinerary maps. They show all the good roads of Europe, with grades, scenic points, distances, gross and intermediate; hotels, policed districts, and many other points, and are used in conjunction with the new European touring book.

E. B.'s interest in automobiles, racing, and traveling continued during this part of his life. But he was also interested in target shooting [clay pigeons] and established the "E. B. Gallaher Trophy" at the Larchmont Yacht Club in 1907. His interests also included boating, specifically sailing on the open waters.

But he continued to show a special interest in French cars. Mark Theobald of "Coachbuilt.com" relates the following story of his interest in one particular car.…."The Brasier".

"The massive and massively expensive chain-drive Brasier was the successor to the Richard-Brasier, which was itself the successor of the Georges Richard automobile.

The Richard-Brasier developed a well-earned reputation after winning the 1904 and 1905 Gordon Bennett Cup [processor to the Grand Prix held annually in Le Mans, France] and despite the fact that Georges Richard left the firm in 1905 to found Unic, the car remained popular despite a name change to Brasier in 1906."

When E. B. decided to withdraw from this business in 1910, Daniel T. Wilson organized the Flandrau Motor Car Co., and took over as importer of the French-built automobile. Wilson served as president of the firm and Manhattan attorney Wilford H. Smith, as vice-president and treasurer.

Flandrau offered twin, four and six-cylinder Brasiers prior to the firm's withdrawal from the US market due to the inherent risk of cross-Atlantic passage due to the developing European conflict.

In addition to a couple of new Brasier chassis, Flandrau inherited E. B.'s stable of used cars and took out classified ads in the <u>Automobile Club of America's Club Journal</u> during 1910.

It was the "Craigslist" of its day and had a wide readership.

Theobold wrote about an advertisement placed by Wilson and Smith of the Flandrau Motor Car Company attempting to generate interest in both the completed and partially compete cars.

"No. 622—1906 Renault. 20-30 H. P., limousine body (Flandrau), convertible into open body with canopy top. Used as town car only. Fine condition. More than fully equipped. Price, $3,500.

Another one stated: **"No. 733— Richard Brasier, 25 H. P., 1906, with two bodies. New touring body by Flandrau, with Victoria hood and slip covers. Limousine by Rothschild, mahogany interior finish. This car will be sold with the two bodies, or with one, or either body will be sold separately. A low figure will be accepted."**

After leaving the hands on automobile business, E. B. went in a new direction and concentrated his energies in developing The Clover Manufacturing Company. He expanded a new manufacturing facility for abrasives. Many of his company's products however were used by the growing automobile industry.

Later he was elected a member of the Board of the Gotham National Bank in New York City.

He took a break from his many business interests and asked his best friend Inez Henry from Philadelphia for her hand in marriage. She accepted and after living for a while in New York City they moved to Norwalk, Connecticut in 1910.

His bride, who was 7 years younger than E. B., was described as a tall striding figure, vibrant with handsome features. They never had children and lived in beautiful surroundings much of their lives.

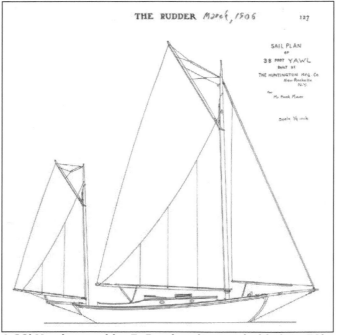

THE RUDDER March, 1906   127

SAIL PLAN
OF
38 FOOT YAWL
BUILT BY
THE HUNTINGTON MFG. Co.
New Rochelle
N.Y.
for
Mr. Frank Meals

Scale ⅛ inch

A 38' Yawl owned by E. B. when he was in his late 50's.

One of the passions he shared with his bride was his continued interest in sailing.

In 1930 he purchased the Tamerlane, a 38 foot yawl built by the Huntington Manufacturing Company in New Rochelle, New York.

Originally built for the Commodore of the New Rochelle Yacht Club, the Tamerlane was an ocean racer. It won the Brooklyn Yacht Club ocean race and was entered in the Brooklyn to Bermuda race.

It is thought that E. B. purchased the boat not for its racing abilities, [he finished third in one race] but for cruising, as it handled very well in the areas around New York and Long Island Sound and was considered a comfortable cruiser.

In 1934, E. B. was elected Commodore of his yacht club in Norwalk, Connecticut. It was a difficult time for the country having just come out of the depression. As Commodore, he scheduled a series of weekly harbor races in an effort to keep morale up in a challenging economic time.

According to the "History of the Rowayton Waterfront", author Karen Jewel noted his accomplishments for the yacht club.

In his effort to keep members informed about the club's status and activities, he put together a newsletter called <u>The Log.</u>

This then led to the club's first yearbook to include a list of all elected officers, the bylaws, and constitution. But the most significant inclusion was a directory of all the yacht clubs from New York to Canada.

E. B. paid for all of these publications out of his own pocket. He later sold his sailing vessel Tamerlane in 1942.

As noted earlier, The Clover Manufacturing Company first organized in New York, became one of the largest employers in Norwalk.

The main products of the company had to do with abrasives to be used in industrial settings.

He also amassed a great number of acres surrounding his Connecticut estate amounting to more than 200. His mansion was grand indeed with stained glass windows, containing many bedrooms and was a great place for entertaining.

Perhaps motivated by the same reasons other inventors tried new ways to do the old better, E. B. added to the list of inventions. He also came up with brand new ideas never tried by anyone.

Ever the handyman when it came to inventions, E. B. designed a "log mover" for his mansion in Norwalk. This contraption allowed an easy way to transfer fire place logs from the basement to the fireplaces in the living spaces of his home.

E. B. designed this hand crank log lift for his home.

The Clover Manufacturing Company eventually became an major player as an international supplier of products.

And according to Plastics Magazine a Ziff Publication, E. B. and his wife Inez were everything but chief, cook, and bottle washer. Here is personnel listing as it appeared sometime in the 1940's.

CLOVER MFG. COMPANY
327 Main Street
Norwalk, Connecticut
Personnel:
I. H. Gallaher, pres.;
E. Y. Gallaher, vice-pres.;
E. B. Gallaher, secy., treas., flen.
mgr., sales mgr. & adv. mgr.;
C. J. Fairhurst, supt. &
plant mar.;
W. G. Beard, chief engr.
dir. plastics research;
M. E. Brown, pur. agent

The "E. Y. Gallaher" noted above as Vice President of the company was E. B.'s younger brother [Ernest] who died in 1959 at the age of 83. Two other siblings died at an early age.

> "I knew Franklin Roosevelt when he was a boy and through his college days – I could tell you lots about him, which, summed up, would be that he was not good then and never was any good during the rest of his life, so when he became President through deception and fraud, I immediately started to fight him in my Clover Letters."

An excerpt from one of The Clover Business Letters

Chapter Eight

E. B. Turns Right

Over the years, as noted, E. B. held most positions in Clover Manufacturing. It was a successful company employing hundreds of workers in its Norwalk, Connecticut base of operations.

Somewhere along the line perhaps in 1922, E. B. began publishing a business oriented newsletter for which subscribers paid an annual fee.

It is reported that he had some 150,000 subscribers at one point, which at $12 per, amounted to 1.8 million dollars annually.

The Clover Business Letter contained a number of information pieces regarding the state of the economy and E. B.'s personal take on the subject.

His political leanings began to go to the far right before World War ll.   In one of his mid-1930's newsletters he even lambasted President Roosevelt.

One of his favorite themes was his opinion that the country was moving toward socialism.   He also was aggressively against the taxes which the government was applying to those that produced wealth.

In 1936, the Federal tax rate for wealthy income producing individuals reached a staggering 75 percent. The top rate was 79 percent which included a "surtax."

This was not something that E. B. took easily as he believed high taxes put a crimp on expanding businesses

E. B. had used his newsletters to express his strong objections to the taxation and the direction the government was taking the country. He was asked by a columnist of the Wyoming, New York newspaper for permission to reprint one of his opinions of the state of the economy. Here is part of the commentary [note that the columnist thought E. B.'s company helped the growers of "clover."]

The Wyoming Reporter, Wyoming, N. Y.
July 24, 1935

Mr. E. B. Gallaher edits a Clover Business Service, published monthly for the information of dealers and growers of clover and allied products, at Norwalk, Connecticut. Subscribers to this service pay $12.00 a year for it and it must be good or they would not pay that price for it in such large numbers. A friend of mine showed me the July1st Issue of that publication and He suggested that I might find some ammunition in it for The Lounge. I wrote Mr. Gallaher asking permission to reproduce his last editorial in Wyoming County Newspapers. He very cordially consented, and here is his last editorial. It would seem that there are other students of finance and economics who feel just as deeply and speak Just as plainly as I do. — THE LOUNGER

WHERE ARE WE HEADING ?

From Clover Business Service

We finally have pure socialism presented to the country by President Roosevelt in his recent tax memorial congress.

Those of us who have been following his actions closely have realized   that his purpose was and is   create a Socialistic State —   scrap the Constitution and to rule the country through a bureaucracy.

The time has arrived for some plain speaking.   It Is not a question of Republican or Democrat — it is now a question of pure Socialism or the Constitution.

We have stated many times that Roosevelt did not want prosperity for the country and never has wanted it; for he knows full well that a prosperous people cannot be socialized. He has known, and knows today that he could have prosperity overnight by simply allowing throttled industry to expand into an enormous ready-made market, which is here and has been here for the past year or more.

In our opinion all this talk by the President about wanting prosperity does not ring true — it is simply a case of throwing dust in our eyes — keeping us guessing while he "takes one step after another to break down our American institutions and to substitute his socialistic theories. His latest soak-the-rich message is pure camouflage — the ORIGINAL purpose was to get a favorable reaction ...."

By 1935, the United States had come out of the depression, but members of the business community were against the "New Deal" promoted by Roosevelt.

They believed he was experimenting with the economy even taking the country off the "gold standard." Deficits in the budgets were looming.

The adoption of "Social Security" resulted in higher taxes on the rich along with new government controls over the banking industry and public utilities. During this same period, those against the politics of the White House decried the effort to spend its way out of debt...by adding more debt through the work relief program for the unemployed.

E. B. continued to rattle the cages of Roosevelt and the federal government though his newsletter. He also sought to establish a program at Yale University which would lay a solid foundation of economic theory.

The theme of his newsletters continued along the same lines for years, as long as the Democrats controlled the White House.

Years later, E. B. had encouraged Yale University, which as mentioned earlier was founded by his grandfather, to adopt a new field of studies.

Michael Holzman wrote a piece entitled "The Ideological Origins of American Studies at Yale." In it he describes the background of funding and direction for the program to be adopted by Yale University.

The connection to E. B. was that he was to contribute a significant sum of money to create a course of study.

Continuing along the same theme he thought that the next great effort must be given to solving economic problems facing the country. And it needed to begin in 1947 so that another half century of progress could be assured for America.

In a letter to the Provost of Yale, E. B. wrote explaining his views that the country was moving in the wrong direction and should encourage strengthening of the free enterprise system.

> *"In my opinion, the present drift toward statism is to be attributed in some measure to the action of [business and financial leaders in the past]. If we are to stop the present trends and to return to a real system of free enterprise, it seems necessary to take some sort of steps to prevent a recurrence of the more serious mistakes made by the powerful figures in the business and financial world."*
>
> *"I have found that you get nowhere if you try to convince people that Socialism is against their best interests if you do not at the same time call their attention to the greed of industry and the financial interests when they are in control."*

His opinionated view of the general population was revealed in a speech made a few years later.

During a speech to the American Ordnance Association in April, 1949, E. B. was quoted as saying:

"The general American population could be divided into percentages with the largest [70 percent] having the intelligence of a 14 year old with half of those in the group being "D-minus" or very low intellect."

"Another 16 percent have 'normal intelligence' but basically initiate little, but can be taught many things and do them well. These 16 percent can acquire a lot of knowledge."

In the "16 per-centers" E. B. noted that this group included small merchants, family doctors, office workers, foremen, and many politicians.

Another group which he indicated made up 9 1/2 percent of the population had high intelligence. This group according to E. B. were the planners, managers and included most of the top executives of companies who are highly educated.

The remaining 4 1/2 percent were thought by E. B., to have high intelligence and included scientists, great doctors, engineers, great business executives and financiers.

His conclusion, based upon this breakdown, was that it wasn't hard to find the causes of the difficulties facing the country. [In 1948 the unemployment rate was only 3.8 percent but shot up to 5.9 percent in 1949 according to the U. S. Department of Labor Statistics].

He categorized the "D-Minus Group" as seeking something for nothing.

In his speech he remarked, *"They realize their inability to do much for themselves; are not impressed too much by their personal freedom or our free enterprise system; are glad to take orders from anyone who promises them security and a living."*

His anti-communist rightist leaning politics then came out in full force when he is quoted as saying, *"Thus, this group of 100 million people has become the prey of the Communists, Socialists, the unscrupulous politician and the labor leader."*

Continuing he is reported to have said, *"These sinister groups of men have promised these poor dupes that they would care for them from the cradle to the grave; all they asked for in return in their votes to keep them in office."*

He did not "Like IKE" for president either, and offered to pay for his physical when Eisenhower indicated a desire to run for President of the United States.

He thought IKE would fail the examination. Robert Taft of Ohio was E. B.'s favorite choice as the Republican nominee against Eisenhower even though he had lost the 1948 nomination to Thomas E. Dewey.

In a closely fought battle in the Republican Convention, Eisenhower won out but later wooed Taft's support of his election campaign against the Democrat and former Illinois Governor Adlai Stevenson.   E. B. would have had a mindset, based on his writings, of being upset that Eisenhower became President.

Some of his diatribes were even placed in Eisenhower's Library in Abilene, Kansas under the heading "Sub Series C Subject File, which according to the Library Catalogue "features several folders of anti-Eisenhower smear materials".

His writings continued through the Clover Business Letters banging the drum for fiscal conservatism and less government intervention in the everyday business and personal lives of the United States.

> *"I further direct that my present home with its 300 acres of land be employed by THE STEVENS INSTITUTE OF TECHNOLOGY as an industrial research center and that a competent director of research be engaged for its development.*

From E. B.'s 1951 Last Will and Testament

CHAPTER NINE

The Later Years

E. B. concluded his Newcomen speech by acknowledging the blessings he and others had in taking part in this amazing opportunity of living in a free enterprise system.

Some fifty-six years after graduating from The Stevens Institute, E. B. received an honorary doctorate from his alma mater. He had been elected a Trustee of The Institute as well.

The date was February 8, 1950, and about the time he was completing his will and making plans to leave his entire estate to the Institute.

His estate included his business, the Clover Manufacturing Company, and also his hundreds of acres private reserve where his 10,000 square foot mansion had been constructed in 1930-31.

Later and as part of the will's direction regarding disposition of his assets, his wife Inez was appointed executrix and would continue to occupy the mansion until her death.

The Gallaher Mansion in Norwalk, Connecticut

E. B.'s interest in donating the mansion and grounds was based on his agreement with the Institute that they would establish a research facility there.

He left his Library to Yale University, which may have included an extensive collection of his Business Letters.

אורים
ותמים

LUX ET VERITAS

YALE UNIVERSITY
LIBRARY

Bequest of

EDWARD B. GALLAHER

A few years after E. B.'s death, his widow was awarded an honorary doctorate from The Stevens Institute. She was only the second woman every to have been awarded this high honor by the Institute.

Inez Gallaher also continued in her role as President of Clover Manufacturing.

Tragedy struck close to home some years later in 1961, as Inez was almost killed in a car accident in Norwalk near the Merritt Parkway.

Her housekeeper was killed in the accident when someone T-Boned her car and Inez was critically injured.

She survived and live another four years and died at age 85 in 1965.

When she died The Stevens Institute took over the Norwalk property and was reportedly to make it a research facility.

A New York Times article in May of 1965 reported that Dr. Jess H. Davis President of the Institute announced its intention of going into the manufacturing of abrasives through the receipt bequest of E. B.

Dr. Davis also noted that the value of the gift [the complete ownership of the Clover Manufacturing Company] was the largest in the history of the Institute and valued in excess of $1 million.

The total gift to Stevens Institute by both E. B. of his Connecticut mansion and acreage and his widow's gift of the Clover Manufacturing stock and property in today's buying power is estimated to be more than $21 Million.

As the Institute's President noted at the time, the bequest was the largest gift in the history of the Institute up to that point.

E. B. left explicit instructions in his will dated September 5th, 1951 that he wanted the property where he lived to be used by The Stevens Institute as a research facility.

His will stated: "I further direct that my present home with its 300 acres of land be employed by THE STEVENS INSTITUTE OF TECHNOLOGY as an industrial research center and that a competent director of research be engaged for its development. My intention would be to have the present large stone house used as an administration building and then to have erected on the surrounding land as appropriate laboratory buildings. My estate should be sufficiently liquid so that there would be money immediately available for the erection of one or more of the laboratory buildings."

For an unknown reason, the Board of Trustees and President decided against carrying out this plan even though E. B. wanted the property to be used by The Institute.

The Institute, after its decision not to create a research center as directed in both E. B. and his widow's wills, sold the property to the City of Norwalk. It is reported that the City paid $900,000 for the estate. The property is now called Cranbury Park and is managed by the City's Parks and Recreation Department.

Today, an association called "Friends of Cranbury Park" a not-for-profit organization works with the City to preserve, protect, and enhance the park.

Efforts to find out about the decision by The Institute to forego the research facility have been for naught. The parties who made the decision are no longer living.

There is no listing of E. B. in the "Notable Alumni" of the Institute as his early achievements and later significant bequest seems to have gone unrecognized.

In the will of Inez Gallaher dated April, 1958 the intention regarding the research facility was also reiterated.

Her will also stated that in the event The Institute did not carryout the establishment of the research facility, her estate was to be given to the Shriner's Hospital in Massachusetts.

According to reports, this medical institution never received any funds from the estate.

The will stated: "..... Thirdly, after a reasonable dividend has been paid, for the establishment and maintaining of an industrial research department in and as part of said Institute for so long as such maintenance shall be deemed by Stevens Institute of Technology, after every reasonable effort has been made by it , to promote its growth an successes, said department to have as its general and other purposed the furthering of an engineering education of the rising generations."

Following these decisions of accepting the estate and the Clover Manufacturing Company, the Institute reportedly named John Wirth to manage the company.

Wirth supposedly later purchased the entire Clover Manufacturing Company including its patents from The Stevens Institute. By 1978, Wirth had the organization running full steam, and even proposed to create an "executive heliport" on the property for executives of other major employers in the area.

In 1986 E. B.'s creation was sold to the Fel-Pro, Inc. of Skokie, Illinois.

The Clover brand is now owned by Loctite a division of the German firm "Henkel" which bought it in 1997.

In his final comments to the Newcomen Society, E. B. left the audience with a positive note but he didn't anticipate the globalization of business commerce.

"May future generations be motivated by the same inspired enthusiasm and by the same dauntless energy which America witnessed during years which we have been examining together. These characteristics have contributed to make America what she is!"

How is his life to be described? There were many opinions of him from readers of his speeches and his newsletters, but there are others who may remember him for his generosity, leadership abilities, and inventiveness.

Each may hold a personal opinion based upon experience or exposure to the man and his beliefs.

He did not forget a number of employees of the Clover Manufacturing Company and directed they be protected upon his death.

His will noted these employees by name, to be assured of a position for at least two years following his demise.

E. B. appeared to be a hard liner politically, but was generous to those around him. His gifts to Yale and The Stevens Institute of Technology indicate that he remembered his roots. His desire to carry on the potential of newer and better ways of doing things through creation of a research facility was tied to his earlier education and opportunities.

He was no doubt an "original car guy" with a seemingly insatiable curiosity for improving the transportation of the late 19th and early 20th Century. His inventions came at a record pace during the years after his graduation.

Patents were filed with the United States Patent and Trademark Office at a continuous rate during E. B.'s lifetime. His early training and mechanical genius served him well through out his career. The story of E. B. Gallaher may fade into history but what will last is the measure of this incredible and "original car guy".

What Is The Measure of A Man?

Is it his passion?
Is it his auto racing abilities?
Is it his quiet sense of humor?
Is it his inventiveness?
Is it his entrepreneurship?
Is it his business leadership?
Is it his charitable deeds?
Is it his accumulated wealth?
Is it his longevity?
Or is it.............

........the lasting measure of a man whose actions gave direction to his many inventions.....who faced business challenges and survived.......who outlasted most of his peers....who gave new meaning to "sage advice"......who also never stopped standing for the principles for which he believed.

E. B. Gallaher certainly gave a new definition to the phrase "The Measure of A Man."

- He will be remembered as an innovator,
- A man with drive and business values;
- A boss with outstanding business leadership and integrity;
- Someone who gave to his community;
- Who set an example of knowing how to accumulate wealth,
- Who also had time to do charitable deeds and share his success;
- A man who shared his life with his lovely and talented wife;

- A man who never lost his sense of speaking freely and sharing his opinions;
- And someone who lived a long full life.

He was also a man who could melt ice with his warm smile and create an icy reception with his incisive writings in The Clover Business Letter.

A man who not only created new ways to do things, but left his legacy of wealth and knowledge to an institution whose purpose is to educate leaders who create, apply and manage innovative technologies while also maintaining a deep regard for human values......The Stevens Institute of Technology.

Edward Beach Gallaher

1873 - 1953
Interred in the Woodlawn Cemetery
The Bronx, New York

Post Script

In 2013 the New Jersey Attorney General's office received an inquiry about the disposition of E. B. Gallaher's estate and the stipulation in his will regarding the bequest to The Steven's Institute.

The inquiry was referred to the Division of Criminal Justice where it is to be reviewed.

As of this publication date, no further information has been provided as to what action if any is to be undertaken by the Attorney General or The Division of Criminal Justice.

Appendix One

Established 1922

 # Clover Business Letter

October 1951
With Supplement

Published Monthly By
E. B. Gallaher, M. E. D. Eng.

For the Customers of
CLOVER MG. CO. NORWALK, CONN.

(Author's Note: The newsletter has been reformatted from two columns per page into the following for readability)

THE AL SMITH SUPPLEMENT TO THIS LETTER SHOULD BE A "MUST" READING

I received a letter, dated July 31, 1951, from Mr. J. N. Mitchell, Central Motor Company, Waco, Texas, which reads as follows:

"I have a considerable advantage over you in at least one respect -- I know you, but you don't know me. I have heard you as a guest speaker address those in attendance at conventions. From the very beginning I was so impressed with the sound logic of your reasoning that I became one of your early subscribers to the "Clover Business Service," the editorials of which I have read with keenest interest throughout the years."

"In looking back through my Clover Business Service files I ran across a Special Supplement captioned, 'Alfred E. Smith's Talk To The American People.' I read it again and it was prophetic in its warning to the American people. I thought so well of it that I paid $35 for 200 photostatic copies, which I will mail out to a selected mailing list.

"I know you are not young any longer, and neither am I, but it is my fervent wish that you may live many more years to preach the gospel of truth."

Turning back to the February 15, 1936, issue of the Clover Business Service, I found the Supplement referred to by Mr. Mitchell, which was a radio talk by Governor Alfred E. Smith when the "Democrats" were about to reelect Roosevelt for a **second** term.

In this speech Al Smith reviews the betrayal of America by Roosevelt and the violation of his oath of office. It is a review of the first four years of Roosevelt's term, during which he set about to eliminate our Constitution, our Bill of Rights, our Supreme Court, and our American system of free enterprise.

As he states, when the "Democratic" platform for Roosevelt's reelection started out by saying, "We, the representatives of the Democratic party in convention assembled, heartily endorse the Democratic Administration" he "took a walk" out of the Democratic Party, into which he had been born. He just couldn't betray his country -- he couldn't become a traitor -- there was no Socialism or Communism in his blood.

Al Smith was one of our greatest American statesman - he was Governor of the great State of New York four times, and ran for the Presidency, being defeated possibly because of his religious leanings.

123

Be that as it may, we can say without fear of contradiction that he would have been a President ten thousand times better than either of the Socialists, Roosevelt or Truman.

Al Smith was absolutely honest - morally honest in the extreme. He had come up from nothing; had absolutely no background, but due to his great vision, love for his country, love for his fellow man, coupled with hard work, absolute honesty and outspoken frankness in all his dealing, he became recognized by the entire world as one of its outstanding characters and was worshipped by all who came in contact with him.

Had the American people only listened to him and thrown this gang of Socialists, Communists, traitors, and grafters out of office in 1936, the country today would not be on the verge of an economic collapse -- we would not now be burdened with a national debt of nearly 260 thousand million dollars, most of which has been created by Truman. We would have no Socialism; we would not have squandered 200 billions abroad.

I knew Franklin Roosevelt when he was a boy and through his college days - I could tell you lots about him, which, summed up, would be that he was not good then and never was any good during the rest of his life, so when he became President through deception and fraud, I immediately started to fight him in my Clover Letters.

When Truman took over at Roosevelt's death, he stated publicly that he assumed the New Deal philosophy in its entirety, so I have been fighting him, the New Deal, later changed to the "Fair Deal" as socialistic, dishonest, subversive and degrading to the American people.

I believe this Al Smith speech, "a voice from the grave," delivered in 1936, to be one of the greatest documents for good government ever produced, because it is the speech of an OUTRAGED DEMOCRAT, against Socialism and Communism which had infiltrated into his old, respectable Democratic party.

And this indictment of the principles and ideals of both the New Deal and the Fair Deal is a challenge to politicians in both the Republican and Democratic parties, who have been betraying the American people and our Constitution in their support of Socialism, wastage, thievery, false propaganda and subversion.

* * * * *

I hope my readers will see the educational importance of this Al Smith speech and will distribute as many thousands of copies as possible, especially to workers and to the man-on-the-street, for Al Smith was the hero of the "underdog" - he was their mouthpiece, always demanding justice for all; his views from the grave regarding the present Government should carry great weight.

I am offering reprints of this talk at less than cost to assure widest possible circulation.

TAXING US OUT OF EXISTENCE

Everything seems rosy to the average person - full employment; all-time high wages; everything we could wish for to buy in our stores; lots of building going on; factories running at full blast; all amusement places and resorts crowded - what have we to fear?

Well, that's just what the fellow thinks when he is sitting on a keg of dynamite smiling a cigarette. It's all right until the dynamite explodes - if he is still alive, he probably wonders what has happened.

We talk of the boom we are in as if it were the natural result of long, hard work, and great and increasing production, made possible by the efforts of everyone, who now are spending their honest earnings, knowing that they have added their share to the productive effort. **But this is all a pipe-dream from smoking the Fair Deal opium.**

We are not in a legitimate boom period - we are on the very verge of an economic collapse. Make no mistake about it!

Some of the money we have been receiving so easily comes to us from government spending, which produces absolutely nothing helpful to the economy. On the contrary, all government spending is a waste - it has added nothing to our national economy and never can.

Another part of the money we get is given to us in many kinds of pensions, the supporting of farmers' prices, unemployment compensation, free housing, social security and countless other give-away programs.

All this money you have been getting has first been taxed away from the seizing of the accumulated wealth of the nation, then to be scattered to the four winds in thousands of give-away programs by our unscrupulous government.

This national wealth, which has taken generations to accumulate, has been the backbone of our industrial strength.   It has financed business; built plants and equipped them; it has given jobs to countless millions of our people; it has been directly responsible for the enormous growth of our nation.

But now our spendthrift government has already stolen most of it, and thrown it away, and our Congress is literally scraping the bottom of the barrel to be certain it gets the last remaining dollar out of those who produce. So, what then?

Well, when our private savings, our fortunes, our accumulations of wealth are gone, then, like it happened in England, we must look to the Government for everything. We have become a socialistic state and we all become slaves of the state, to do as we are told - or else!

Well, it may come as a shock, but when our Congress gets through with its present taxing program we will have reached practically the end.

And this new taxation is so unnecessary, because all experts agree that ten billion dollars could easily be cut from he President's budget without interfering in the slightest in the operation of the government, plus our rearming program.

The question asked by the man-on-the-street is: "If this is true, why doesn't Congress cut the budget by ten billion before it ever considers new taxation?" A perfectly fair question.

The reason is that a majority of the members of Congress are cowards. They know perfectly well that the cuts could and should be made - off the record they openly say so.

But when it comes around to cutting some absolutely worthless, pork-barrel item where the money is to be spent in their state or district, they cease to be honest men, working for the good of the whole nation, and, fearing for their own reelection, they hustle about to get pledges of support from other members of Congress to prevent the cutting of their little pet scheme which they want as an ace-in-the-hole when elections come around.

Now, when we realize that this illegitimate, pork-barrel spending exists in most states in the union, naturally most Senators and Representatives have axes of their own to grind. So, when one legislator asks another to support his pet graft, the answer is, "O.K., but you must agree to support my pet graft." There you have it.

The majority of those in Congress are not statesmen; they are cheap politicians, who think first of themselves and their personal advantage, and care little what happens to the country.

We will never be able to cut these huge budgets, loaded with graft, until the people begin to flood Congress with protests, as they did in the case of General MacArthur.

What we need are not a few thousand letters written to the Congress; we need millions of them telling our representatives that we want economy in government spending - or else! They know what the "or else" means, and if enough people write and telegraph, they will do as they are told.

An aroused country is the only cure for the present dangerous spending spree.

FOR RELIEF FROM OUR PRESENT TAX BURDEN
NEW AMENDMENT TO THE CONSTITUTION

The country has become so overburdened with federal taxes during the post-war period that the American people are in open revolt.

The taxes the federal government has collected since the end of the war haven't been used for arming the country, nor has the money been spent for any purpose beneficial to the country.

The bulk of the money collected since the end of World War II -- **a period of peace in the nation** -- has been squandered, thrown away, used for payroll padding, misappropriated or used for handouts and giveaway programs in order to buy votes to maintain the Fair Deal in power.

Federal thievery through taxation has become so bad that our states find it difficult to obtain money for their normal and proper operations, so have been forced to go to the Administration for small sums to help 08t -- **these small sums representing only tiny fractions of the money pillaged from the people and the instructress of our states.**

Apparently the only way to restrain our spendthrift government is through an amendment to the Constitution which would limit the take of the federal government to a definite amount.

To put this in force a joint resolution was adopted by Congress, which would limit federal income tax rate to 25 per cent. This bill was introduced by the Honorable Noah M. Mason of Illinois.

The joint resolution must be ratified by three-fourth of all the states before it becomes part of the Constitution. Already 25 states have ratified it, and it needs only 11 more before it becomes law.

Every taxpayer should do all in his power to have his state ratify this joint resolution, and every state official should exert all his influence to get it adopted.

This act would immediately check the national government from its socializing activities; thus, states would find it easier to finance themselves when the burden of federal taxation is lightened for its citizens.

Let's get busy and get the job done!

DOES THE FAIR DEAL WANT INFLATION?

Evidently the Fair Deal boys feel it would be a good political move for them to start a runaway inflation now, let it run along for a few months, then apply the many controls they have up their sleeves to check the inflation just before the 1952 elections and go before the voters as saviors of the people from ruinous inflation.

At least it seems to me to be a good guess that this is taking place, for what other reason can be given for DiSalle and others in the Administration putting their high-power propaganda machine to work, telling us that prices are going up from 5 to 10 per cent; that goods will be scarce and hard to get, when, at the present time and for the foreseeable future, prices seem to have reached their peak and are declining; inventories held by manufacturers, wholesalers and retailers are at their peak; manufacturers are slowing down production of consumer goods for lack of orders -- this doesn't look like higher prices!

This is not the first time inflation has been caused by false information being given by our officials in order to gain something for themselves politically -- the last time they did it, at the start of the Korean war, it was to scare the people and the Congress into giving them added controls and more spending money.

One thing it has taught the country is the absolute unreliability of any and all statements made by the Fair Deal stooges -- you just can't believe a word they say.

Today there is little danger of runaway inflation, unless the public falls for the high pressured propaganda now going on, which seems unlikely, as people are getting wise; nor are there any signs that Russia will attack us -- at least for several years.

THE U. N. -- AMERICA'S BOSS

In my Clover Letters of January 1949 and June 1951, I wrote on the dangers of America remaining as a member of the U. N.

When we were drawn into the U. N. through high-handed government propaganda, the idea of having all the countries in the world united in common defense against aggression in the world seemed so plausible that many were carried away with the thought without first subjecting the whole proposition to a careful analysis of what our responsibilities would be, and staging an open discussion as to whether a world government would be desirable of America or no -- **for the U. N. is in fact a world government.**

131

We entered the U. N. with a treaty, duly passed by Congress and signed by the President.

Now, under the Constitution of the United States, a treaty supersedes all the present laws of our land and any laws we may later enact; any of our Supreme Court rulings, and any laws or court rulings by any and all of our states became null and void if they interfere with the carrying out of the orders of the U. N. under the present treaty.

Since the U. N. was formed, it has spread out its functions in many other directions besides simply keeping the peace, and it now proposes to expand its activities in many new directions, all of which will involve using world government at the expense of our own freedom.

The U.N. is dominated today by Socialists and Communists, though we are paying 40 per cent of the total cost of its operations.

IN OTHER WORDS, BY SIGNING A TREATY WITH THE U.N., WE HAVE GIVEN UP OUR CONTITUTIONAL RIGHTS TO RUN OUR OWN AFFARIS AS WE SEE FIT, and must now go to the U.N. for permission to do as we please under our Constitution and our own laws.

This whole thing seems so absurd that most people would laugh at the idea as being nonsense -- but it is a fact.

The U.N. is the brain-child of a bunch of irresponsible Socialist ad Communist sympathizers in our own Government, who have always had the wild idea that there should be a world government in absolute control of all countries, and they have used the enormous American propaganda machine to sell their idea through the world.

There is evidently a defect in our Constitution which should be promptly amended to PROVIDE PROECTION FROM CONGRESS MAKING A TREATY WITH A FOREIGN STATE WHICH WOULD THEN BECOME THE LAW OF THE LAND IN AMERICA, SUPERSEDING ALL OUR PRESENT LAWS.

It should be noted that while a treaty binds America to recognize it as the law of the land under our Constitution, the same treaty, signed by other countries, does not bind them in a similar manner.

A fast one has been put over on us by our Socialist Government, which has bound the country hand and foot without most of us knowing that our Constitutional liberties have been taken away from us. The Socialists are certainly slick operators.

I believe two things would be done at once to protect American independence: (1) a joint resolution, as suggested, amending our Constitution, should be introduced in the Congress at once and sent the states for ratification, and (2) we should withdraw from the U. N. at once, as its various actions in recent years have shown conclusively that this group of foreign Socialists and Communists, who are dictating to us, are no friends of our country.

The U. N. is a good example of what can happened when we fail to heed the warnings given us by our Founding Fathers to "avoid foreign entanglements."

TRUMAN AND STALIN

For several years I have closely watched the moves made by Stalin, first to confuse, then frighten, then crack down and take over his intended victims.

He has followed a well-defined Communist formula, which is at long last beginning to be understood by the man-on the-street in all countries -- therein, by the way, lies hope.

I presume many of my readers are also trout fishermen; those who are know that if you really want to catch a trout, you must take it easy. If you cast rapidly in the same pool you frighten the fish, because they become suspicious. If you hook a big fellow, much confusion has been created in the pool in landing him; you should then fish elsewhere until things quiet down.

Well it is the same thing when you start fishing for something in a pool of human beings. If you get too active you are likely to fail. You have to do your accumulating, bit by bit, until you get the whole thing.

Now Stalin has been doing just that and he has accumulated plenty in many parts of the world in the last four or five years.

I have also watched Truman since he became President, and I find that he and his Socialist advisors have been following the Communist line in Stalin's footprints; only, instead of fishing for world domination, Truman and his Commissars are after complete control of the United States.

Over the past years, bit by bit, the Congress has been asked to give up the Constitutional rights of the people, which could only have been accomplished because members of Congress, always keeping their ear close to the ground, have felt that the people wanted it that way -- many are unscrupulous politicians, only seeking reelection. Had they been statesmen they wouldn't have done it.

The reason people have fallen for Socialism is because of the continuous high-pressure propaganda, **costing many millions in tax money each year, over a period of 20 years,** which has drugged them into believing they would be better off to have the Government support them than to stand on their own two feet and fight it out themselves. People have also been moved by the fact that, if they were to work hard and save for their old age, their money, already half value, would likely be worth so little in another ten years that it would not be worthwhile.

It is this combination, taken out of the Marxist book, which has nearly done the trick in America: (1) destroy the value of our money so that savings become worthless, then (2) have the Government step in, offering support and all kinds of promises of something-for-nothing.

In any event, when we analyze the Stalin method and the Truman method, we cannot help being impressed that they are practically identical, even though their ambition for quiet conquest is somewhat different.

Truman is continually attacking Stalin for political effect; likewise, Stalin is attacking Truman for the same reason. Isn't it a case of the pot calling the kettle black? Are they not both trying to do the same thing?

WEST POINT SCANDAL

What can we expect from the cadets of West Point when their Commander-in-Chief condones stealing, lying and all forms of subversive activities in his official family and in his own Government, then openly protects the culprits?

We are all sorry to see these 90 cadets dismissed for infraction of the "honor system" existing at the Academy, but what could be more natural when they see the honor system fall apart among their superiors?

What can you expect when they see their Commander-in- Chief and members of the top brass violating their oath of office? Read the oath and see what you think:

"I do solemnly swear (or affirm) that I will faithfully execute the Office of ...., and will, to the best of my ability, preserve, protect and defend the Constitution of the United States."

It is just too bad that there is not an enforceable "honor system" existing within the national Government -- if there were, a large number of those in the Administration and in Congress would have been expelled long, long ago. In Washington the word "honor" has not existed since Roosevelt was elected 20 years ago.

And, by the way, this same lack of morals, lack of common honesty, failure to speak the truth, grafting, lack of loyalty to the Constitution which has existed for 20 years, and still exists in the very highest places in all three branches of the Government, is entirely responsible for the degradation of moral fiber of the entire country, the reaction being: if the top men in the country think it's all right to graft, steal, lie or support enemies of the country, why isn't it all right for me to do the same thing?

Naturally, we are all shocked at this exposure, but look around you in your own community and you will see the effects of immorality in high places very generally reflected in the attitude of the youth of the nation.

STEALING THE OTHER FELLOW'S THUNDER

If it weren't so tragic it would be funny to see the little fellow in the White House and his "Edgar Bergen" going to San Francisco to attend the signing of the treaty of peace with Japan, which was negotiated entirely by General MacArthur.

As soon as MacArthur was fired, a State Department stooge was sent to Japan "to arrange for a treaty of peace". **What bunk! The treaty of peace had been agreed upon and was ready for signature before the stooge left America!**

Now MacArthur's treaty of peace with Japan is ready for signature -- MacArthur is not invited to attend the meeting. Oh, No! This would focus public attention on his great accomplishments!

The gang which has been leading the country to destruction now wants to become the "dove of peace" in the eyes of the nation; so, in order to detract attention from their private Korean war, their many failures in Europe, and their many war scares, they are trying to steal the glory of peace-maker from General MacArthur -- it won't succeed; the people are completely wise and won't fall for this cheap political trick.   Truman and Acheson would command more respect if they stayed at home.

E. B. Gallaher

* Clover Mfg. Co. --Since 1903. Manufacturers of Clover Lapping and Grinding Compounds and a full line of Abrasive Papers and Cloths.   The circulation of the Clover Business Letter is restricted to our customers and those within the business range of our company. To get on the list, send for a file card.

*Due to the great number of request for the Clover Business Letter from those outside of our business range we are offering this group a $2 yearly subscription partially to cover printing, postage and handling.

*EXTRA COPIES: We are always glad to send, with our complements, a few additional copies of thee Clover Business Letter to readers who may desire them. In case a number of copies are desired, please remit your order at the rate of 2 cents per copy to avoid bookkeeping.

Appendix Two

Newcomen Society
of the United States

From Wikipedia, the free encyclopedia

"Actorum memores simul affectamus agenda."

("We look back but go forward.")

The **Newcomen Society of the United States** was a non-profit educational foundation for "the study and recognition of achievement in American business and the society it serves." It was responsible for more than 1,600 individual histories of organizations, from corporations to colleges, which were distributed to libraries and its membership.

English origins

It was patterned after the Newcomen Society of Great Britain, founded in London in 1920, a learned society formed to foster the study of the history of engineering and technology.

Both groups took their name from Thomas Newcomen (1663-1729), the British industrial pioneer whose invention of the atmospheric steam engine in 1712 led to the first practical use of such a device -- lifting water out of mines.

Newcomen's invention helped facilitate the birth of the Industrial Revolution. He is frequently referred to as the "Father of the Industrial Revolution."

The Newcomen Society in North America

The Newcomen Society of the United States began as The Newcomen Society in North America, founded at New York City in 1923 by Leonor F. Loree, then dean of American railroad presidents, together with a group of other prominent business leaders.

The original members were nominated from leaders in business, industry, education, military and other professions.

Its declaration of purpose was to:
- Preserve, protect and promote the American free enterprise system.
- Honor corporate entities and other organizations, which contribute to or are examples of success attained under free enterprise, and to recognize contributions to that system.
- Publish and record the histories and achievements of such enterprises and organizations.
- Encourage and stimulate original research and writing in the field of business history through a program of academic awards, grants and fellowships. [4]

Established soon after the ascent of communism in the Soviet Union, The Newcomen Society in North America championed American capitalism, material civilization and entrepreneurship.

But the English and American branches together counted only 323 members in 1933, the year leadership for The Newcomen Society in North America went to its co-founder and Loree's friend, Charles Penrose, Sr. (1886-1958). A graduate of Princeton University with a career in engineering, Penrose found a new calling at Newcomen.

Declining a salary, he became senior vice-president when the presidency was largely honorary, and under his dynamic governance the society achieved stature and prestige. He started sectional committees and aggressively recruited as member's industrialists, educators, bankers and businessmen.

Membership soared to 12,000, while the British chapter numbered less than 500.

In the late 1940s, Penrose built the society's headquarters on Newcomen Road in rural Exton, Pennsylvania.

It was complete with a 2,700-volume library and museum featuring a range of antique model steam engines operated by hand cranking or electricity. Beside a chapel stood a bell tower, which played a carillon.

Designed by the Philadelphia architect Briton Martin (1899-1983), the campus had offices, guest houses and a printing shop for Newcomen Publications, Inc which Penrose founded to produce the society's distinctive illustrated booklets featuring company histories.

At Seapoint Beach in Kittery Point, Maine, the society maintained a summer retreat with guest cottages.

Penrose appeared to know personally the top executives of every major company in the United States, and by charisma and will, made Newcomen an important part of their lives.

Called a "benevolent despot," he oversaw every detail on the society's production line of tributes to organizations, from editing and publishing an average of 55 booklet histories per year, to officiating across the country at 60-70 luncheons and dinners annually at which the histories were orated by their authors.

Except for educators, expenses were usually paid by the enterprises being honored, which bought for distribution over 12,000 copies to enhance their reputations.

It is no exaggeration to say that, in its heyday, anyone who was anyone in American commerce, manufacturing and academia belonged to the Newcomen Society in North America.

In 1952, *Time Magazine* referred to Penrose as "a combination of P. T. Barnum and the Archbishop of Canterbury."

It quoted him saying:
> *"We are attempting to hold up to America the vision and the courage and the hard work and abiding faith -- make that a capital F -- of the men who years ago created the America which we have inherited."*

Charles Penrose, Sr. died suddenly in 1958, the year he finally became president. The chairmanship next went to his son, Charles Penrose, Jr. (1921-2007). By 1981, The Newcomen Society in North America had 17,000 members.

Decline

Following the retirement of Charles Penrose, Jr., a succession of directors lacked the zeal and vision, which had driven captains of industry to found Newcomen.

Despite its mandate to promote engineering and technology, Newcomen's clubby rituals seemed dated in the age of the Internet and video conferencing. In a struggle to survive, Newcomen sold the Exton campus and its sumptuous furnishings.

Its collection of antique model engines was auctioned by Christie's in 2001. But to no avail -- on December 17, 2007, Chairman Daniel V. Malloy and the trustees announced that The Newcomen Society of the United States would close due to declining membership.

Over its 84-85 year existence, it honored more than 2,500 organizations and institutions.

The archive of Newcomen Society histories is preserved at The National Museum of Industrial History in Bethlehem, Pennsylvania.

In 2007, the chairman and trustees announced the society's closure.

ABOUT THE AUTHOR

An award winning screenplay writer and author of books on a variety of subjects, djv murphy spent most of his adult life working in the not-for-profit sector. His involvement with eleemosynary organizations allowed him to gain a variety of life experiences serving as inspiration to his writing.

Of Canadian parentage, he has lived on both the West and East Coasts of the United States as well as in the Midwest.

Along the way, he developed a keen interest in the arts, and after early retirement from his position as President of an international charitable organization, Murphy began his second career in the creative field.

He started by designing and winning awards for historic building renovations.

Murphy then opened a combination art gallery and restaurant, which exhibited the art work of more than 200 artists from around the world, including his own linear abstract works, and turned to writing award winning screenplays and books.

He resides on a farm in rural New Jersey and is past president of The Canadian Club of New York [now Canadian Association of New York], Trustee Emeriti of the Morris Animal Foundation, member of the Penn Club of New York, Harvard Writers Group, and various film and trade associations.

His works may be found on Amazon.com and BarnesandNoble.com and in selected bookstores. His personal website for books and screenplays is www.djvmurphy.com

Made in the USA
Middletown, DE
15 November 2016